SHERIDAN

H O R

STUDIES IN LITERATURE

General Editor: Penny Gay

Jane Austen's
EMMA

Penny Gay

Senior Lecturer in English
University of Sydney

SYDNEY
UNIVERSITY PRESS

SYDNEY UNIVERSITY PRESS
in association with
OXFORD UNIVERSITY PRESS AUSTRALIA

© Penny Gay 1995
First published 1995

This book is copyright. Apart from any fair dealing for the purposes of private study, research, criticism or review as permitted under the Copyright Act, no part may be reproduced, stored in a retrieval system, or transmitted, in any form or by any means, electronic, mechanical, photocopying, recording, or otherwise, without prior written permission. Enquiries to be made to Oxford University Press.

Copying for educational purposes
Where copies of part or the whole of the book are made under section 53B or section 53D of the Copyright Act, the law requires that records of such copying be kept. In such cases the copyright owner is entitled to claim payment. For information, contact the Copyright Agency Limited.

National Library of Australia
Cataloguing-in-Publication data:

Gay, Penny
Jane Austen's Emma.
Bibliography.
ISBN 0 424 00207 8.

1. Austen, Jane, 1775–1817. Emma.
(Series: Horizon studies in literature).
I. Title.
823.7

Cover illustration by Jiri Tibor Novak
Printed in Australia by Australian Print Group
Published by Sydney University Press in association
with Oxford University Press,
253 Normanby Road, South Melbourne, Australia

CONTENTS

GENERAL PREFACE

More often than not, set texts for high school and undergraduate students seem overly familiar: the reader's relationship with them is tired. Although it is probably true that all authors hope their works will become 'classics', they would never intend them to become tiresomely familiar. The aim of this series of short critical studies is to *refresh* students' and teachers' readings of these books, by offering detailed close analysis allied to an overview informed by recent trends in criticism and scholarship.

Literary criticism is never static; what seemed important to say about a work twenty or fifty years ago will seem glaringly obvious, or irrelevant, to us today. This is because our own perspective or way of viewing the world limits and defines our reading, especially our reading of the past (even the recent past). The critical endeavour should be to make our 'horizon' meet the horizon of the work, the author's world. Neither cancels out the other, but what the work 'says' to us depends on the questions that we think are relevant to ask about it. The text remains a classic because modern readers can gain both meaning and pleasure from their reading of it.

It is hoped that students will find these studies liberating, by encouraging them to ask new questions of their set texts, in providing them with new information about the writer's world (both historical and imaginative), and in directing them to techniques of critical reading that they may not yet have encountered. The ultimate aim of this series is to expand the reader's horizon.

Penny Gay
English Department, University of Sydney

FOREWORD

All quotations from Jane Austen's novels are taken from the editions published in the World's Classics series, Oxford University Press. These editions reproduce the idiosyncratic spellings of early nineteenth-century printers. Quotations from *Emma*, edited by James Kinsley, are from the 1990 reprinting of the World's Classics edition, but for ease of reference the chapters have been renumbered continuously rather than retaining the original three-volume format.

Robert Gay drew the hypothetical sketch map of Highbury, having reread the novel with scrupulous care in order to pick up Jane Austen's 'clues' to the topography of her imaginary world. For his commitment to this project I am most grateful.

Thanks are also due to Jill Lane of Sydney University Press for her enthusiastic and well-informed support of not only this volume but the Horizon series of which it forms a part.

EMMA'S WORLD

Naming the heroine

'What two letters of the alphabet are there, that express perfection?'
asks Mr Weston at a painfully inappropriate moment on the ill-fated
expedition to Box Hill. The answer is a 'gratifying' pun on Emma's
name, 'M. and A. — Em–ma' (p. 336). It is in fact 'a very indifferent
piece of wit', but, coming at this crucial point in the novel, it reminds
the reader of much more than the immediate psychological and moral
situation. Games of all sorts — verbal games, parlour games, the games
of social behaviour — are a continual theme in Emma's life, and in the
novel that tells her story. This study is an attempt to plumb Jane
Austen's own 'game' with the reader as she constructs the tale of 'a heroine whom no one but myself will much like'.[1]

'Emma' is the heroine of a novel — a crafted fiction — and takes her
place among others in a literary line: Richardson's *Clarissa* and *Pamela*,
Burney's *Evelina*, *Cecilia*, or *Camilla*, or *Belinda* (by Maria Edgeworth)
as Austen herself remarks in *Northanger Abbey*, Chapter 5. That is,
there was already a tradition in the novel, a literary form not yet a century old, of focus on the life of a woman. The question implicit in all
these novels is, what are the possibilities of a woman's life in a world
organised according to the desires of men? For the female members of
the gentry, are the only choices a single life of frivolity, domestic

respectability as some man's wife, and the literal or metaphorical death that results from 'dropping out' of one's proper class? In *Emma* we see examples of all three of these possibilities, with Jane Fairfax's half-hidden and potentially tragic story illustrating the last.

Austen's novel is a comedy rather than a tragedy (like Richardson's *Clarissa* (1749) which tells the story of the abduction, rape and death of the heroine), and Austen's typically ironical mode of storytelling implicates the reader almost as much as the heroine in a wry narrative of the dismantling of illusions. By telling the story almost entirely from Emma's point of view, Austen obliges us — if only on our first reading — to experience vicariously the discoveries about herself and about life that Emma makes in the course of the narrative. But it is also a novel which expects the reader to be a re-reader, because it guarantees us the pleasure of enjoying the author's craft(iness), watching the manipulation of character, noting the clues to Jane and Frank's 'hidden' story and the interweaving of themes. The novel is both a 'Moral Tale' such as Maria Edgeworth wrote, and a sophisticated game.

A map of the world

When Austen begins this novel with the words 'Emma Woodhouse, handsome, clever, and rich, with a comfortable home and happy disposition, seemed to unite some of the best blessings of existence', the sophisticated reader will register a slight, if amused, unease at that verb *seemed*. Undoubtedly the novel is going to focus on this young woman, but what is going to happen to her to turn her 'seeming' into reality? In the second half of the opening sentence we read that she 'had lived nearly twenty-one years in the world with very little to distress or vex her'. She is thus about to attain her majority; this will be a novel about becoming an adult. But by the time we've read to the end of Chapter 1 we also realise that 'the world' in which Emma lives so comfortably is comically small:

> Highbury, the large and populous *village almost amounting to a town*, to which Hartfield, in spite of its separate lawn and shrubberies and name, did really belong, afforded her no equals. (p. 5, my emphasis)

In fact, despite the magisterial declaration of Austen's editor R. W. Chapman — 'the indications are *just* not sufficient' (Collected Edition, p. 521) it is possible from the clues given throughout the novel to draw a map of Highbury, although the village cannot be

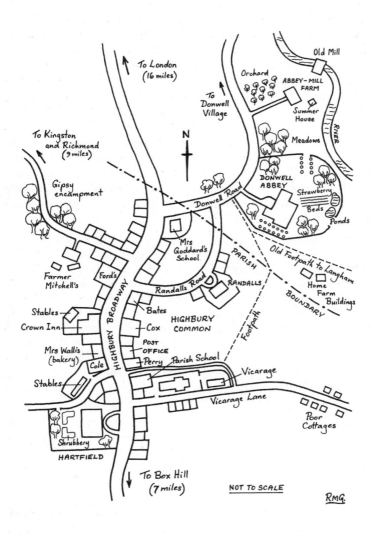

A hypothetical map of Highbury in Surrey, including part of the
Parish of Donwell

identified with any 'real' place ('no possible place is at once sixteen miles from London, nine from Richmond, and seven from Box Hill', says Chapman; perhaps we may think of Highbury as existing in an 'alternative universe'). The hypothetical map on page 3 shows that Jane Austen *imagined* the place as a self-contained, real though small world: Randalls is half a mile from Hartfield, Donwell a mile away in the neighbouring parish; the real Kingston-on-Thames, eleven miles to the north, is the market town; and the real beauty spot Box Hill is seven miles away from the fictional Highbury. (Jane Austen stayed at Great Bookham in Surrey — in the area of the fictional Highbury — in June 1814, having begun *Emma* in January of that year.) We can easily imagine the position of Mrs Goddard's small school, with its 'ample house and garden'; of Ford's emporium in the High Street; of the church and the vicarage, and Farmer Mitchell's of Broadway Lane. The fictional town of Highbury is richly peopled with minor characters and their activities. One of Emma's most positive characteristics is her ability much of the time to be satisfied with this small community, which represents the parameters of her own life:

> Much could not be hoped from the traffic of even the busiest part of Highbury; — Mr Perry walking hastily by, Mr William Cox letting himself in at the office door, Mr Cole's carriage horses returning from exercise, or a stray letter-boy on an obstinate mule, were the liveliest objects she could presume to expect; and when her eyes fell only on the butcher with his tray, a tidy old woman travelling homewards from shop with her full basket, two curs quarrelling over a dirty bone, and a string of dawdling children round the baker's little bow-window eyeing the gingerbread, she knew she had no reason to complain, and was amused enough; quite enough still to stand at the door. A mind lively and at ease, can do with seeing nothing, and can see nothing that does not answer. (pp. 209–10)

But again the sting in the prose lies in the final, apparently commendatory, remark: by this stage in the novel we should recognise that Emma's 'mind lively and at ease' is all too likely to turn the material closest to hand — the everyday life of Highbury — into the fables of an 'imaginist' (p. 302): 'nothing that does not answer' means 'everything can be used for my needs'.

What, indeed, is Emma to do with her abundant energy and lively mind in a place as small and unchallenging as Highbury? The question might have been asked of themselves by hundreds of Jane Austen's young women readers, caught in a round of making calls on their neighbours, practising their 'accomplishments', and charitably visiting the poor of the parish. Emma's problem, as the first chapters make clear, is that she is surrounded by uncritical admirers of her energetic personality: Miss Taylor, the teacher who became a mother-substitute, 'had such an affection for her as could never find fault' (p. 4); her 'indulgent' father, who 'could not meet her in conversation, rational or playful' (p. 5); Harriet Smith, the girl dragged out of her own class and its activities ('moonlight walks and merry evening games' (p. 24) with the Martin family) to be Emma's plaything.

There is only one character in the novel with an energy equivalent to Emma's (excluding Frank Churchill, who is febrile rather than energetic). That is of course Mr Knightley, who strides into the first chapter's depressed and diminished Hartfield bringing a breath of fresh air from the outside world. He replies heartily to Mr Woodhouse's fear that he 'must have had a shocking walk' with:

> 'Not at all, sir. It is a beautiful, moonlight night; and so mild that I must draw back from your great fire.'
> 'But you must have found it very damp and dirty. I wish you may not catch cold.'
> 'Dirty, sir! Look at my shoes. Not a speck on them.' (p. 8)

And it soon becomes clear that here is the person who *can* meet Emma in conversation, both rational and playful, as they energetically disagree over the merits of Emma's match-making activities. By the end of Chapter 1, the sophisticated reader will have registered the unmistakable signals of an attraction which neither protagonist is yet willing to recognise, and the outline of a plot that will teach Emma a lesson about her belief that she can direct other people's lives.

One of the most remarkable things that the hypothetical map shows is the extent of Mr Knightley's property: he *owns* almost all of the land shown. 'The landed property of Hartfield certainly was inconsiderable, being but a sort of notch in the Donwell Abbey estate, to which all the rest of Highbury belonged...' (p. 123). He also owns the land surrounding Donwell (off the map), including the Abbey Mill Farm of which Robert Martin is a tenant. Thus many of the characters in the novel will be Mr Knightley's tenants — even those living in Highbury, with the exception of those who have been able to buy houses, as Mr Weston did the 'little estate' of Randalls (p. 13). Mr Knightley is a property-rich man. But we are also told that he had 'very little spare money' (p. 191); it is obviously all ploughed back into the estate rather than spent on personal luxuries (for example, he never takes a carriage when he can walk or ride on horseback).

Food, sickness, and health

Like Elizabeth Bennet of *Pride and Prejudice*, Emma is a heroine in the perfect 'bloom of full health' (p. 34). Mrs Weston is given a speech (in colloquy with Mr Knightley, who confirms the suspicions raised in Chapter 1 by saying 'I love to look at her') which insists on the reader's noticing this, not just inferring it from her abundant energy:

> '… such a pretty height and size; such a firm and upright figure. There is health, not merely in her bloom, but in her air, her head, her glance. One hears sometimes of a child being "the picture of health"; now Emma always gives me the idea of being the complete picture of grown-up health.' (p. 34)

What a clear contrast this presents with the picture of her father, the hypochondriacal Mr Woodhouse! Once again, the reader is brought to consider what Emma might *do* with this abundant vitality, in a society which allows the useful expression of energy only to men. That it is a more restrictive society than that of the earlier *Pride and Prejudice* is indicated by the difference between Elizabeth's walk 'alone' to Netherfield — 'crossing field after field at a quick pace, jumping over stiles and springing over puddles with impatient activity' (*Pride and Prejudice*, p. 28) — and Emma's timidity about walking alone to Randalls: 'it was not pleasant' (p. 22). For all her vitality, Emma is virtually immobilised in Highbury: her sense that she is 'fixed, so absolutely fixed, in the same place' (p. 129) as the importunate Mr Elton is an expression of a deeper claustrophobia which no doubt is the subconscious reflection of her life with her father. Mr Elton, however, being a male, takes advantage of his gender superiority to ride off to Bath and find another young lady to woo. Elizabeth, by contrast, travels to — and encounters her lover in — Kent and Derbyshire, as well as flitting about her home county. Emma, like the daughter of another wealthy house, Maria Bertram of *Mansfield Park*, is trapped in her social position and its expectations ('that iron gate, that ha-ha, give me a feeling of restraint and hardship. I cannot get out, as the starling said', Maria says as she fumes over the limitations of her fiancé, the stupid but rich Mr Rushworth (*Mansfield Park*, p. 89)).

As John Wiltshire has pointed out in his fascinating study, *Jane Austen and the Body*, the question of physical health — particularly that of women — is of continual interest to Austen.

The bodily condition of these heroines is not an isolated factor in the play of meanings these novels entertain. If the healthy body is largely passive, unconscious of itself, then the unhealthy body, as a site of anxious self-concentration, is the source of events, of narrative energies.[2]

Wiltshire touches briefly on the role that food plays in this focus on the body, but I should like to examine in more detail the pattern that can be drawn from a list of the food mentioned (eaten or refused) in the novel. First, Mr Woodhouse's denial of the body and its pleasures — including, we might infer, sex, since sexual union and fertility is what the wedding symbolises:

the wedding-cake, which had been a great distress to him, was all ate up. His own stomach could bear nothing rich, and he could never believe other people to be different from himself. What was unwholesome to him he regarded as unfit for anybody; and he had, therefore, earnestly tried to dissuade them from having any wedding-cake at all, and when that proved vain, as earnestly tried to prevent anybody's eating it. (p. 16)

The late *Mrs* Woodhouse, we assume, must have been a woman who insisted on her marital rights! Her younger daughter, though infantilised by living with her father — to the point that she believes herself not subject to sexual desire — does appreciate the other pleasures and needs of the body:

with the real good-will of a mind delighted with its own ideas, did [Emma] then do all the honours of the meal, and help and recommend the minced chicken and scalloped oysters which she knew would be acceptable to the early hours and civil scruples of their guests. (pp. 20–1)

Mr Woodhouse can only recommend to his guests 'such another small basin of thin gruel as his own' while nervously offering his advice about eggs 'boiled very soft', '*very* little bit[s]' of apple tart, and not advising the custard.

In Volume Two Emma sends 'the whole hind-quarter' of a porker to the needy Bates family, while Mr Woodhouse again worries about the 'wholesomeness' of the meat, though 'thoroughly boiled … and eaten very moderately of, with a boiled turnip, and a little carrot or parsnip', it is acceptable to the stomach (if dull to the palate). Mrs Bates, however, loves a hearty roast loin of pork, and the family has already partaken of it, with accompanying baked apples (p. 153 ff.). Mrs Bates and Mrs

Goddard are the victims of Mr Woodhouse's dietary tyranny on the night of the Coles' dinner-party: Emma 'had provided a plentiful dinner for them; she wished she could know that they had been allowed to eat it' (p. 191). The meal at the Coles' is *not* described — since attitudes to food have no symbolic significance here. On a later occasion again poor Mrs Bates is deprived of one of her favourite foods, 'a delicate fricassee of sweetbread and some asparagus ... good Mr Woodhouse, not thinking the asparagus quite boiled enough, sent it all out again' (p. 297).

The Bateses are also looked after with gifts of food from Mr Knightley — in fact the last of his stock of apples, which they have baked as something to tempt the almost anorexic Jane Fairfax ('she really eats nothing — makes such a shocking breakfast, you would be quite frightened if you saw it' (p. 213)). And when they themselves are visited by Emma, they insist that she take some sweet-cake: 'Mrs Cole had just been there, just called in for ten minutes, and had been so good as to sit an hour with them, and she had taken a piece of cake, and been so kind as to say she liked it very much; and, therefore, she hoped Miss Woodhouse and Miss Smith would do them the favour to eat a piece too' (p. 138).

Old Mrs Bates, the silent member of the Bates household, is in many ways the focus of this theme of the need and desire for palatable food. She functions as a symbolic representation of the basic body — with no extra advantages such as youth, beauty, wit, or masculinity. The undeniable fact of our embodiedness must be acknowledged and given its due if the novel is to fulfil its claim to represent the concerns of everyday life. Mrs Bates plays no active role in the plot or 'romance' of the novel, but she is *there*, a silent figure who emphasises the ordinary reality of the Highbury world. 'Dear Jane,' as Miss Bates says in the fullness of her heart at the sight of the Crown ball supper-table, 'how shall we ever recollect half the dishes for grandmamma? Soup too! Bless me! I should not be helped so soon, but it smells most excellent, and I cannot help beginning' (p. 297).

Why this focus, and why is the novel so fascinated by details of food offered, eaten or refused? Perhaps Austen wishes to make a further point: that it is the *gendered body* which exists in the world. The Bateses (and Jane) are powerless and near-indigent women: their welfare literally depends on the generous impulses of the energetic and well-off. Jane virtually goes on a hunger strike when it looks as though she will have to accept the job with the friends of the Sucklings which Mrs

Elton has officiously organised. The novel also makes us aware that this gendering is an unfair division of society when one such as Emma, who has such a strong awareness of the body and its needs and capabilities, is limited in her productive service to the community — while on the other hand, Mr Woodhouse's position is deferred to although he denies the body and its pleasures and needs, simply because he is a male. Emma's abundant vitality and good health, and her position as virtual head of the Hartfield household, give her a factitious power in the novel; whenever possible she overrides Mr Woodhouse's denials of food and pleasure. She will find the true outlet for her energy as the chatelaine of Donwell Abbey, whose owner, as an active farmer, is the principal producer of food in the community. We see him discussing animatedly with his city-based brother 'the plan of a drain, the change of a fence, the felling of a tree, and the destination of every acre for wheat, turnips, or spring corn' (pp. 90–1), and his dependence on his daily chats with his steward, William Larkins, about the management of the Donwell estate, is the subject of some teasing by Emma (see below, p. 40).

This estate, as the turnips might suggest to those who know their history,[3] is a product of the eighteenth-century Agrarian Revolution: land cleared and amalgamated through the various Enclosure Acts of the previous two centuries now cultivated by new scientific methods of farming and crop rotation. The 'poor cottagers' whom Emma visits in Chapter 10 are a passing acknowledgement of the unfortunate side-effects of the enclosures which destroyed the traditional strip-farming of the peasantry: their only source of income now would be as labourers. Already in 1815 in the north and Midlands the even more dramatic Industrial Revolution was making its mark and radically changing the social hierarchy and physical appearance of England. But Austen's novels are set in the conservative southern counties, in which a landowner might still, at this point in history, present an image of good stewardship — as Mr Knightley consistently does.

Games

Mr Knightley is the visitor to the Hartfield drawing-room who makes the backgammon table, with which Emma had been hoping to 'get her father tolerably through the evening', 'unnecessary'. This is the first of the games, both small and large, with which the inhabitants of the novel while away their time and energy. The backgammon board is here clearly figured as merely something to fill up the time before sleep, delivering its players from boredom and querulousness — and none of the novel's other games deviate from this connotation. Observe, for example, the heavy irony with which the narrator records

> the only literary pursuit which engaged Harriet at present, the only mental provision she was making for the evening of life, was the collecting and transcribing all the riddles of every sort that she could meet with, into a thin quarto of hot-pressed paper, made up by her friend, and ornamented with cyphers and trophies.
>
> In this age of literature, such collections on a very grand scale are not uncommon. Miss Nash, head-teacher at Mrs Goddard's, had written out at least three hundred ... (p. 63)

The 'friend' who is assisting Harriet in this infantile exercise is her mentor and social superior, Miss Woodhouse — a far cry from the intentions of 'improving her little friend's mind, by a great deal of useful reading and conversation'; and although Emma herself is not charmed by the foolishness of a riddle-collection, she is happy to take the opportunity to play her own game, 'let[ting] her imagination range and work at Harriet's fortune' (p. 62). Mr Elton, who should be employed fulfilling his parish duties — including the thoughtful writing of the weekly sermon — demeans his position by joining in the trivial game of riddles. When the smirking gentleman brings a riddling verse for Harriet's collection, thinking thereby to woo Emma, his handiwork is contrasted disparagingly by Harriet with the plain 'good sense' of Robert Martin, who does his wooing by 'sit[ting] down and writ[ing] a letter, and say[ing] just what you must, in a short way' (p. 69). This is also the sensible practice of the novel's hero, Mr Knightley, when he finally declares his love to Emma: 'I cannot make speeches, Emma. ... If I loved you less, I might be able to talk about it more' (p. 390). But Mr Elton knows all the right speeches to make in the social game of courtship.

Frank Churchill is also never at a loss for the acceptably elegant speech; and he is of course the novel's most consummate game-player. We shall consider the qualities and functions of his game-playing in a later chapter, but it is worth noting here that as Emma reflects on the disastrous Box Hill party at which 'Mr Frank Churchill and Miss Emma Woodhouse flirted together excessively' (that is, played at mutual sexual attraction for the benefit of the audience) she thinks of it, after Mr Knightley's rebuke has reduced her to tears, as a morning more completely misspent, more totally bare of rational satisfaction at the time, and more to be abhorred in recollection, than any she had ever passed. A whole evening of back-gammon with her father, was felicity to it. (p. 341)

ROMANCE VERSUS REALITY

Emma's romance about Harriet

To play a game is to enter into a world of unreality, to behave *as though* the premises of the game were real. Writing or reading a novel clearly comes under this heading, and Austen was always aware that she was treading on this seductive but dangerous ground. In *Northanger Abbey* (one of her earliest-written books, but published after her death) the heroine, seventeen-year-old Catherine, is seduced by her reading of the Gothic novels of Mrs Radcliffe into imagining that her host at the Abbey has imprisoned or even murdered his wife. As the hero Henry Tilney says when he realises to what absurd lengths Catherine's imagination has taken her,

> 'If I understand you rightly, you had formed a surmise of such hor-
> ror as I have hardly words to — Dear Miss Morland, consider the
> dreadful nature of the suspicions you have entertained. What have
> you been judging from? Remember the country and the age in
> which we live. Remember that we are English: that we are
> Christians. Consult your own understanding, your own sense of the
> probable, your own observation of what is passing around you —
> Does our education prepare us for such atrocities? Do our laws

connive at them? Could they be perpetrated without being known in a country like this, where social and literary intercourse is on such a footing, where every man is surrounded by a neighbourhood of voluntary spies, and where roads and newspapers lay everything open? Dearest Miss Morland, what ideas have you been admitting?' (p. 159)

Emma, a self-professed 'imaginist' (p. 302), is not aware of the dangers of this activity, and her mentors, Mr Knightley and Mrs Weston, are too busy with their own lives to give her more than occasional warnings (as Mr Knightley does in Chapter 1). For much of her story she plays the game of 'author' of the life of Highbury, so we have a story about a person who makes up stories about the lives of the people in a country village. Thus does Austen deconstruct the apparent 'reality' of her own writing.

Novels by women — or 'romances' — usually focus on the adventures and trials of a heroine. The stereotyped figure of just such a young girl, straight out of the popular novel of Jane Austen's youth, presents herself to Emma in Chapter 3:

> Harriet Smith was the natural daughter of somebody. Somebody had placed her, several years back, at Mrs Goddard's school, and somebody had lately raised her from the condition of scholar to that of parlour-boarder. This was all that was generally known of her history...
>   She was a very pretty girl, and her beauty happened to be of a sort which Emma particularly admired. She was short, plump and fair, with a fine bloom, blue eyes, light hair, regular features, and a look of great sweetness. (p. 19)

Emma, determining 'to continue the acquaintance', tells herself, '*She* would notice her; she would improve her; she would detach her from her bad acquaintance, and introduce her into good society; she would form her opinions and her manners'. How easy is the slide from patronising and helping this young woman to *authoring* her, 'forming' her! No wonder Emma concludes her musings with the thought that thus to take over Harriet's life would be 'interesting ... highly becoming her own situation in life, her *leisure*, and *powers*' (p. 20, my emphasis). Emma needs employment for her leisure and her power of creative imagination; her 'situation in life' gives her another sort of power, more morally questionable. So the discomfiting story of Emma's manipulation of Harriet's emotional life is played out, until at last she realises that if indeed Harriet has succeeded in attracting the affections of Mr Knightley, Emma must bear the consequences in honourable silence: 'Who had been at pains to give Harriet notions of self-consequence but herself? — who but herself had taught her, that she was to elevate herself if possible, and that her claims were great to a high worldly establishment?' — as invariably befalls the heroines of conventional romance (p. 376).

The novel's single most 'romantic' incident is the adventure of Harriet and the gipsies (Chapter 39). Gipsies are a standard motif in the popular Gothic fiction of the late eighteenth and early nineteenth centuries. They are exotic nomads, their lifestyle everything the contrary of respectable Englishness, and their abduction of the blue-eyed heroine is almost to be expected. The fact that they were also a common feature of the early nineteenth-century English countryside is a useful tool in Austen's satirising of Emma's tendency to romanticise ordinary reality. Like the poor parishioners whom Emma and Harriet visit in Chapter 10, they are a sign of the social facts surrounding the comfortable lives of the country gentry (Mr Knightley, as chief landowner and magistrate, needs to be informed 'of there being such a set of people in the neighbourhood', p. 301). The experience for Harriet herself is clearly frighteningly real:

> Harriet was soon assailed by half a dozen children, headed by a stout woman and a great boy, all clamorous, and impertinent in look, though not absolutely in word. — More and more frightened, she immediately promised them money, and taking out her purse, gave them a shilling, and begged them not to want more, or to use her ill. — She was then able to walk, though but slowly, and was moving away — but her terror and her purse were too tempting, and she was followed, or rather surrounded, by the whole gang, demanding more. (pp. 300–1)

But for Emma, safely ensconced in Hartfield, the sight of an evidently agitated Harriet leaning on the arm of her rescuer Frank Churchill is easily read as romantic. Harriet obligingly 'sink[s] into a chair and faint[s] away' as soon as she enters the house, unconsciously (so to speak) fulfilling the role of romantic heroine ('For an Hour & a Quarter did we continue in this unfortunate Situation — Sophia fainting every moment & I running mad as often' wrote the young Jane Austen in her hilarious burlesque of popular fiction *Love and*

Freindship [sic]). Emma, as soon as she has with her sensible side attended to the immediate needs of the situation, begins to revel in the 'adventure' thus presented to her imagination:

> Could a linguist, could a grammarian, could even a mathematician have seen what she did, have witnessed their appearance together, and heard their history of it, without feeling that circumstances had been at work to make them peculiarly interesting to each other? — How much more must an imaginist, like herself, be on fire with speculation and foresight! (p. 302)

Now, the professions of linguist, grammarian, and mathematician are real professions in the real world; they base their conclusions on scientifically observed phenomena. But Emma has invented a profession for herself, and its name: the word *imaginist* is a nonce-word invented by Austen (*OED*).

Emma is not, in fact, a very good 'writer' — probably because she has never got very far with the lists of books that she has for years been setting herself to read (the chief way a woman of her class, like Austen herself, could get education beyond elementary schooling and young ladies' accomplishments): as she contemplates Harriet's adventure her language takes on the quality of Harriet's vapid exclamations:

> It was a very extraordinary thing! Nothing of the sort had ever occurred before to any young ladies in the place, within her memory; no rencontre, no alarm of the kind; — and now it had happened to the very person, and at the very hour, when the other very person was chancing to pass by to rescue her! — It certainly was very extraordinary! (p. 302)

This is the language of intellectual poverty, which Anne Radcliffe, the finest Gothic writer of the period (and much admired by Austen), would never stoop to. Yet some version of it becomes 'the story of Harriet and the gipsies' which Emma must daily recite to her young nephews, who 'tenaciously set her right if she varied in the slightest particular from the original recital' (p. 303). Emma, it seems, can tell a good children's adventure story, but she is under-equipped to deal with adult feeling and motivation.

The event that Emma embroiders on as 'extraordinary' is, in fact, perfectly explicable in realistic terms; but it requires the keen mind of a reader of detective fiction (a form yet to be invented) to pick up all the clues that Austen's narration blandly lets fall. Frank is in a position to rescue Harriet because of the agenda underlying his every action:

The pleasantness of the morning had induced him to walk forward, and leave his horses to meet him by another road, a mile or two beyond Highbury — and happening to have borrowed a pair of scissars the night before of Miss Bates, and to have forgotten to restore them, he had been obliged to stop at her door, and go in for a few minutes: he was therefore later than he had intended; and being on foot, was unseen by the whole party till almost close to them. (p. 301)

Even, we might consider, the cramps which prevent Harriet from following the example of her companion, who with unladylike agility 'ran up a steep bank, cleared a slight hedge at the top, and made the best of her way by a short cut back to Highbury' (p. 300), were the effect of Frank Churchill's insistence on the ball at the Crown Inn, so that he could spend time in Jane's company. The irony is that the ball has encouraged Harriet to imagine her own romance — the Cinderella story of the lowly young girl who is noticed by the man of principal importance at a ball: Mr Knightley's 'rescuing' of her from the social embarrassment of not having a partner is quite sufficient material for *her* romantic imagination to work on.

When Emma finally realises the error of her ways in trying to 'arrange everybody's destiny' (p. 374), she turns from a romance author to something much closer to Jane Austen's own mode of ironic realism. It occurs to her that 'it would be inexpressibly desirable to have [Harriet] removed just now for a time from Highbury, and — indulging in one scheme more — ... it might be practicable to get an invitation for her to Brunswick Square ... a few weeks spent in London must give her some amusement' (pp. 395–6). Austen as author has the last laugh, of course, and arranges the plot so that Harriet will meet again her first love Robert Martin who, like Harriet, has momentarily escaped the confines of Highbury and Donwell parishes for the amusements of the big city. Emma could not have dared to imagine this romance of ordinary life!

The games of social life

Harriet Smith is not the only pawn of Emma's unruly imagination. Jane Fairfax, a member of her own class — and therefore not so amenable to the crude manipulations Emma uses with Harriet — is also an orphan in an interesting and slightly mysterious situation. Even before meeting Jane after her two years' absence from Highbury, Emma has imagined her role in a vulgar romance: of being a possible threat, with her greater beauty, to Miss Campbell's marriage. When she does meet her again, Jane's genuine 'distinction, and merit' oblige Emma to rewrite her imagined romance in a high-minded tragic mode: 'If it were love, it might be simple, single, successless love on her side alone. She might have been unconsciously sucking in the sad poison, while a sharer of his conversation with her friend; and from the best, the purest of motives, might now be denying herself this visit to Ireland.' (pp. 149–50) But when Frank Churchill arrives on the scene soon after Jane's own arrival, he — a much more sophisticated and committed game-player than Emma — encourages her to elaborate heights of fancy on the subject of Jane's supposed love for Mr Dixon, thus providing the perfect smokescreen for his own affair with Jane.

It must be said in fairness to Frank that he only builds on a foundation freely supplied by Emma. The occasion of his beginning this game is the Coles' dinner party (Chapter 26). This is one of Austen's brilliant set pieces, in which a number of members of the community are brought together on a social occasion during which the novel's plot and themes are significantly advanced while apparently nothing more profound than idle chatter goes on. It is worth examining this chapter in some detail as an example of Austen's typical technique.

Frank has apparently been to London on a whim to have his hair cut, which is the occasion for Emma to 'moralize to herself', against Mr Knightley's imagined strictures, that he is *not* a trifling, silly young man' (p. 190) since he is not behaving like a coxcomb or a coward. She is only partly right: second-time readers know that his real mission has been to order the piano for Jane; not the action of a trifling or silly young man, perhaps, but certainly that of an egotistical and thoughtless one. The implicit contrast is made explicit within two paragraphs, as Emma arrives at the Coles' to find Mr Knightley also arriving in a carriage, a rare event for him, since 'having little spare money and a great deal of health, activity, and independence, [he] was too apt, in Emma's opinion, to get about as he could, and not use his carriage so often as became the owner of Donwell Abbey' (p. 191). It emerges much later in the course of the evening (and not by his announcing it) that he has employed his carriage for the generous and thoughtful purpose of conveying Miss Bates and Jane to and from the party. Emma's conversation with him as they arrive is a good example of the linguistic energy and competence that they share (as was evident in the novel's very first chapter), and contrasts with the smart one-liners of her later conversation with Frank in this chapter (see below):

'This is coming as you should do,' said she; 'like a gentleman. I
am quite glad to see you.'

He thanked her, observing, 'How lucky that we should arrive at
the same moment; for, if we had met first in the drawing-room, I
doubt whether you would have discerned me to be more of a gentleman than usual. You might not have distinguished how I came
by my look or manner.'

'Yes, I should; I am sure I should. There is always a look of consciousness or bustle when people come in a way which they know to
be beneath them. You think you carry it off very well, I dare say;
but with you it is a sort of bravado, an air of affected unconcern; I
always observe it whenever I meet you under those circumstances.
Now you have nothing to try for. You are not afraid of being supposed ashamed. You are not striving to look taller than anybody
else. Now I shall really be very happy to walk into the same room
with you.'

'Nonsensical girl!' was his reply, but not at all in anger.

(pp. 191–2)

Emma, in her relationship with Frank, partakes of fantasy and play-
acting — 'guessing how soon it might be necessary for her to throw
coldness into her air; ... fancying what the observations of all those
might be, who were now seeing them together for the first time' (pp.
190–1) — while that with Mr Knightley, as we see here, is familiar,
warm and comfortable.

The Coles, we have already been told, are very anxious that this
party should be a success, and that Miss Woodhouse should not regret
her condescension in accepting their invitation. It is Mrs Cole's social
gaucherie which encourages the gossip about Jane's mysterious present,
and when Austen gives us a sample of her speech in her own voice, we
are forcefully reminded of the social and cultural limitations of
Highbury:

'I declare, I do not know when I have heard anything that has given
me more satisfaction. It always has quite hurt me that Jane Fairfax,
who plays so delightfully, should not have an instrument. It seemed
quite a shame, especially considering how many houses there are
where fine instruments are absolutely thrown away. This is like giving ourselves a slap, to be sure; and it was but yesterday I was telling
Mr. Cole I really was ashamed to look at our new grand pianoforte
in the drawing-room, while I do not know one note from another,
and our little girls, who are but just beginning, perhaps may never
make anything of it; and there is poor Jane Fairfax, who is mistress

of music, has not anything of the nature of an instrument, not even the pitifullest old spinet in the world, to amuse herself with.'
(p. 193)

No wonder Emma is attracted to the suave and sophisticated Frank; Austen moves momentarily into dramatic form as we read their three-page dialogue, totally without markers indicating which of them is speaking or qualifiers as to the manner of their speech. This is the heartlessly clever dialogue of the theatre of Jane Austen's youth — Sheridan's *School for Scandal*, for instance — and it is a clear signal to the reader that Emma and Frank are 'playing', literally as though they were in a theatrical comedy. The absence of speaker attributions suggests that their 'real' personalities, with all their emotional complexities, are temporarily in abeyance. Frank is the more knowledgeable player, and he performs his ingenuous role to perfection. As Emma reminds him of the romantic circumstance of Mr Dixon's saving Jane from falling overboard, saying 'If I had been there, I think I should have made some discoveries,' Frank can reply with an irony unnoticed by any but the second-time reader, 'I dare say you would; but I, simple I, saw nothing but the *fact*, that Miss Fairfax was nearly dashed from the vessel and that Mr Dixon caught her' (p. 195). And the second-time reader may well imagine the malicious pleasure with which Frank concludes the exchange:

'Indeed you injure me if you suppose me unconvinced. Your reasonings carry my judgment along with them entirely. At first, while I supposed you satisfied that Colonel Campbell was the giver I saw it only as paternal kindness, and thought it the most natural thing in the world. But when you mentioned Mrs. Dixon, I felt how much more probable that it should be the tribute of warm female friendship. And now I can see it in no other light than as an offering of love.' (p. 196)

After the flirtatious excitement of this quasi-theatrical performance — ending, significantly, on a note of erotic tension (it is Frank who uses the daring word *love*) — it is no wonder that Emma's consciousness registers the rest of the party's 'usual rate of conversation' as depressingly provincial: 'nothing worse than every day remarks, dull repetitions, old news, and heavy jokes' (pp. 196–7), and that the narrator's sympathy seems to be with her in this generalisation. But in the following paragraph Emma has picked up Frank's taboo word and begun to embroider a more extravagant fantasy on it, a fantasy involving the concept of 'the dangerous pleasure of knowing [one]self beloved by the husband of [one']s friend' (this from sensible, lively Emma, normally content with the offerings of Highbury high street!). Emma feels herself 'too much in the secret' of Jane's guilty love to want to speak to her (which might, perhaps, have cooled these hothouse fantasies), but watching her from afar, she sees Jane blush when the gift of the piano is mentioned, and reads the blush according to her own scenario: it is a 'blush of consciousness' followed by a 'blush of guilt' (though blushes do not come in identifiably different varieties). By the end of the next short paragraph, Emma believes that she can 'plainly read in the fair heroine's countenance' her inner feelings; but what strikes the reader is that Jane Fairfax has now become in Emma's creative imagination the 'fair heroine' of a cheap romance novel.

Emma, by Chapter 34, is conscious that somebody or something is playing a game with *her*, that the Jane Fairfax who she thinks to be the property of her romance is incomprehensible:

'She is a riddle, quite a riddle! … She must have some motive, more powerful than appears, for refusing this invitation [to join the Dixons] … she must be under some sort of penance, inflicted either by the Campbells or herself. There is great fear, great caution, great resolution somewhere. — She is *not* to be with the *Dixons*. The decree is issued by somebody. But why must she consent to be with the Eltons? — here is quite a separate puzzle.' (p. 257)

Here Emma attempts to reinstate Jane as the heroine of a Gothic novel; but in fact it is she, Emma, who is using the language of the intrepid but naive protagonist of the Gothic: this speech is most reminiscent of Catherine Morland as she considers the contents of the mysterious chest in *Northanger Abbey*. The author of this mystery, this riddle, this puzzle, is of course Frank Churchill.

Returning to our examination of the Coles' dinner-party, we see that what Emma cannot now read correctly, because of her determined placing of Jane as the heroine of a different romance, is the attention Frank pays to Jane as the evening progresses. He 'pay[s] his compliments en passant to Miss Bates and her niece' (p. 198) on returning to the drawing-room, 'look[s] intently' at her when Emma is otherwise engaged (p. 199), and then turns his momentary embarrassment to his advantage by proposing to go over and ask Jane if her hairdo is 'an Irish fashion' (p. 200), placing himself 'improvidently' in front of Jane so that Emma 'could absolutely distinguish nothing' of their colloquy.

(Later we read that he has 'found a seat by Miss Fairfax', p. 204.) With superb dramatic irony Jane Austen now sets up a conversation between Emma and Mrs Weston, in which it appears that Mrs Weston has momentarily become an 'imaginist': 'In short, I have made a match between Mr Knightley and Jane Fairfax. See the consequence of keeping you company!' (p. 201)

Emma is so shocked by this prospect that she does not 'see the consequence' and apply its lesson to herself. Her repeated exclamation, 'Mr Knightley must not marry!' and her overprotesting appeals to the rights of 'little Henry' offer an amusing insight into the true state of her own feelings, both about Mr Knightley and about the real person 'Jane Fairfax', no longer the fair heroine of a romance, but the prospective mistress of Donwell Abbey and thus the woman of highest status in the community: 'every feeling revolts'. With keen psychological insight, Austen shows us that Emma's emotional confusion at this point pushes her to the relief of mimicking Miss Bates, a comic foreshadowing of her moment of cruel mockery on Box Hill. At the same time, this passage shows us the genuine vitality of Emma's imagination — not at all unlike her creator's — for what Emma gives us here is a 'scene' for Miss Bates from a hypothetical sequel to the Highbury story:

> 'To have her haunting the Abbey, and thanking him all day long for his great kindness in marrying Jane? "So very kind and obliging! But he always had been such a very kind neighbour." And then fly off, through half a sentence, to her mother's old petticoat. "Not that it was such a very old petticoat either — for still it would last a great while — and, indeed, she must thankfully say that their petticoats were all very strong."' (p. 203)

Emma, when she is truly grown up, might yet be able to write comic novels in the style of Jane Austen, rather than the tawdry romances of her youth.

The Coles' evening party ends with music. Emma sings, and is unexpectedly joined by Frank's second part, 'slightly but correctly taken' (p. 204). This of course sets up a situation in which he can openly and naturally duet with Jane — 'They had sung together once or twice, it appeared, at Weymouth' (p. 205), and as 'the sweet sounds of the united voices' accompany her thoughts she reverts to consideration of the prospect of Mr Knightley's marriage with Miss Fairfax. The subtext of the conversation that then takes place between herself and Mr Knightley as he seats himself by her is Emma's testing of her instinctive knowledge of his character and personality: he is obviously of much greater importance to her than the specious Frank Churchill is. And his care for the welfare of others — in this case, the obviously tired Jane Fairfax — is strongly contrasted (in front of Emma) with the egotistical and selfish Frank, who wants Jane to go on singing with him.

It is nevertheless the gamesman Frank who still has the upper hand at the end of this long and complex chapter of social interaction. He secures Emma 'with most becoming gallantry' for the first of the impromptu waltzes. Emma looks to check whether Mr Knightley has similarly secured Jane — but Mr Knightley, 'no dancer in general', is yet to make his move into that most symbolic of mating rituals in Jane Austen's fiction. When he does so, at the Crown ball, his 'gallantry' is first properly directed at rescuing Harriet from embarrassment, and then, climactically, he and Emma agree to dance together.

'Whom are you going to dance with?' asked Mr Knightley.
She hesitated a moment, and then replied, 'With you, if you will ask me.'
'Will you?' said he, offering his hand.
'Indeed I will ...' (p. 298)

But that chapter ends before we can see how well they dance together. The earlier chapter, however, ends with Frank's malicious and deeply misleading remark to Emma, 'I must have asked Miss Fairfax, and her languid dancing would not have agreed with me, after your's.' The second-time reader might well wonder if we can hold out any hope for a relationship based, it seems, more on a perverse attraction than the harmonious union of bodies and like-thinking minds.

ENGLAND VERSUS FRANCE

Who *is* Frank Churchill? Chapters 42 and 43 of the novel — the expeditions to Donwell and Box Hill — are orchestrated by Austen so as to 'place' Frank precisely in the novel's moral and indeed allegorical scheme. These chapters are another two examples of Austen's skill in manipulating her preferred form of narrative: the interactions of '3 or 4 families in a Country Village' (*Letters*, no. 100) during one of their social gatherings. But beyond this, Donwell and Box Hill themselves have a symbolic significance: the one a place of order, stability, and productivity, the other a place for the frivolous and unstructured wanderings of people with nothing better to do — the Eltons, particularly, despite their supposed pastoral role in the community. The fact that 'Emma had never been to Box Hill' (p. 318), although it is only seven miles away from Highbury, suggests that even she has better things to do with her time (looking after her father, playing first lady of Highbury) than emulating 'the bustle and preparation, the regular eating and drinking, and pic-nic parade of the Eltons and the Sucklings' (how the mention of the offstage 'Sucklings' makes pigs of the 'regular eating and drinking' here alluded to!). Her discomfort at Mr Weston's inclusion of the Eltons in the plans for the excursion is not snobbery but her well-founded 'very great dislike of Mrs Elton' which she knows that Mr Weston is aware of; the 'the unmanageable good-will of [his] temper' (p. 319) lacks true thoughtfulness. Even small communities need to organise themselves with discrimination.

Mr Knightley's chivalrous proposal that the party come to Donwell and eat his ripening strawberries is taken up by Mrs Elton and turned into a full production number, with herself playing the role of 'Lady Patroness' (p. 320). Exactly how she imagines herself as Lady Patroness is a matter of some significance:

> '... It is to be a morning scheme, you know, Knightley; quite a sim-
> ple thing. I shall wear a large bonnet, and bring one of my little bas-
> kets hanging on my arm. Here — probably this basket with pink
> ribbon. Nothing can be more simple, you see. And Jane will have
> such another. There is to be no form or parade — a sort of gipsy
> party. We are to walk about your gardens, and gather the strawber-
> ries ourselves, and sit under trees; and whatever else you may like to
> provide, it is to be all out of doors; a table spread in the shade, you
> know. Everything as natural and simple as possible. Is not that your
> idea?'
> 'Not quite. My idea of the simple and the natural will be to have
> the table spread in the dining-room. The nature and the simplicity
> of gentlemen and ladies, with their servants and furniture, I think is
> best observed by meals within doors. When you are tired of eating
> strawberries in the garden, there shall be cold meat in the house.'
> (pp. 320–1)

To a contemporary reader of the novel, Mrs Elton's theatrical fantasies associate her not only with the socially problematic gipsies, the ill-behaved rabble (see above, p. 15), but even more radically, with the foolish behaviour of Queen Marie Antoinette of France, whose play-acting with her ladies-in-waiting at being milkmaids — even having a complete imitation rustic 'hamlet' built for the purpose at Versailles — was one of the elements which provoked the French populace into its revolutionary struggle for liberty, equality, and fraternity. In 1793, when Jane Austen was eighteen, the French King and Queen were guillotined. The aristocratic husband of one of Austen's cousins suffered the same fate in 1794. Mrs Elton, by casting herself in the role of the frivolous aristocrat, is behaving in a way that might contribute to the breakdown of the traditional good order of English society.

The well-ordered hierarchical society of the English countryside is represented by Mr Knightley, as is clear from his correction of Mrs Elton's fantasy with a realistic observation of 'the nature and the simplicity of gentlemen and ladies, with their servants and furniture'. Mrs Elton is not to be put off her fantasy, however, and elaborates it, now moving to the mode of sentimental French and Italian genre paintings with the vision of herself and friends on donkeys, 'my caro sposo walking by' (p. 321).

By contrast, the image that Donwell supremely presents is that of Englishness: Englishness as a moral force that can effortlessly withstand the disruptive challenges of such upstarts as the pseudo-cosmopolitan Mrs Elton. Importantly, the reader's first impression of Donwell is given through Emma's eyes, and it is a measure of her imminent arrival at maturity, though there is still a vein of Austen's irony running under her rendition of Emma's thoughts, giving them a double meaning that Emma cannot yet recognise:

> She felt all the honest pride and complacency which her alliance with the present and future proprietor could fairly warrant, as she viewed the respectable size and style of the building, its suitable, becoming, characteristic situation, low and sheltered; its ample gardens stretching down to meadows washed by a stream, of which the Abbey, with all the old neglect of prospect, had scarcely a sight — and its abundance of timber in rows and avenues, which neither fashion nor extravagance had rooted up. The house was larger than Hartfield, and totally unlike it, covering a good deal of ground, rambling and irregular, with many comfortable, and one or two handsome rooms. It was just what it ought to be, and it looked what it was; and Emma felt an increasing respect for it, as the residence of a family of such true gentility, untainted in blood and understanding. (p. 323)

This country house, significantly named 'the Abbey' — that is, having a direct connection to a centuries-old spiritual tradition by being built on the site and from the fabric of a religious edifice — is *respectable, suitable, becoming, characteristic, sheltered, comfortable*, with *ample* gardens and *abundant* timber. It pays no heed to the *fashion* of contemporary landscaping fads, with their concern for picturesque 'prospects'. It is literally conservative: 'neither fashion nor extravagance had rooted up' its 'abundance of timber in rows and avenues'. And it has no truck with play-acting: 'It was just what it ought to be, and it *looked what it was*.' Emma's and Austen's own political conservatism here coincide in a panegyric on the notion of '*true* gentility, untainted in blood and understanding'. The implication of the novel is that the purity of the old gentry-class is disappearing, and that the Sucklings and Bragges — *the nouveau-riche* of this first century of bourgeois dominance of society — are drawing uncomfortably close. Mrs Elton is, after all, present with the happy couple in the novel's last paragraph.

Mrs Elton continues to demonstrate her failings as a proper member of the gentry in her strawberry-gathering monologue and her effusion to Jane about the prospect of 'a most desirable situation' with a cousin of Mrs Bragge. Both speeches are represented by Austen as being linguistically uncontrolled and poverty-stricken: the first descending quickly from hyperbole to peevishness ('glaring sun — tired to death — could bear it no longer'), the second only represented by the clichés of Mrs Elton's own snobbery: 'Delightful, charming, superior, first circles, spheres, lines, ranks, every thing' (p. 324). Even Jane's exemplary patience is tried by this vulgar persistence, and at her suggestion, the party walks about the grounds of the Abbey.

Here occurs the second passage within two pages in which Austen's patriotic conservatism is plainly declared. We look at Donwell now not from Emma's point of view, with the attendant ironies, but from the perspective of a narrator with distinct political commitment to an ideal image of the English countryside. The walkers, hot, scattered and dispersed, are 'insensibly' drawn to 'the delicious shade of a broad short avenue of limes': the Abbey and its grounds seem imbued with natural magic — or the remnants of that spiritual power implicit in its name. Again the narrator stresses a disdain of fashionable 'taste' in the organisation of the landscape; instead she offers a fortuitous 'extremely pretty' view — the view of the Abbey Mill Farm, 'favourably placed and sheltered' within a natural English landscape, 'with meadows in front, and the river making a close and handsome curve around it'. This prospect, in which the gentleman-landowner's Abbey and fruitful grounds embrace in their purview the farm on which a more general national productivity is based, is, the narrator declares,

> a sweet view — sweet to the eye and the mind. English verdure, English culture, English comfort, seen under a sun bright, without being oppressive. (p. 325)

When Austen in the next paragraph, returning to Emma's point of view, allows her to admire this pastoral landscape with the agriculturally inaccurate 'rich pastures, spreading flocks, orchard *in blossom*' (this is midsummer: the orchard ought to be in leaf and young fruit), we know that she is offering her readers, totally without irony, a vision of an ideal order that can still be imagined in England's green and pleasant land.[1]

That ideal community can be shaken, though, by what Frank and Jane represent in the novel. Jane's encounter with Emma, as she precipitately leaves the Abbey, is the clearest picture we have yet been given of the desperate situation of young women such as Jane who are not protected, as Emma is, from the realities of their society by family and fortune. 'Miss Woodhouse, we all know at times what it is to be wearied in spirits. Mine, I confess, are exhausted' (p. 328). Between the well-meaning supervision of her aunt and the officiousness of Mrs Elton Jane can find no space for her own 'spirit' to flourish — that much is clear to Emma, and she is sensitive enough to sympathise and watch Jane 'safely off with the zeal of a friend'. What she does not know, of course, is the additional strain Jane is suffering under because of her secret engagement to Frank Churchill. The second-time reader will add in this factor, and also the inference that when Frank arrives some quarter of an hour later, 'out of humour', he has met and quarrelled with Jane in Donwell Lane.

Like Mrs Elton, Frank cannot bear the heat of the summer day (yet we have been told that the sun was not 'oppressive') — cannot, shall we say, cope with the moral authority embodied in Donwell. Emma offers him some refreshment, thus recalling for us her role in the novel's deployment of the eating and drinking motif and associating her prophetically with the role of hostess of Donwell Abbey. Frank is so much improved by this as to be able to 'talk nonsense very agreeably', to resume his flirtatious mask. What we hear him say, however, is something more pernicious than 'nonsense'. In the context of this chapter's discourse of England and Englishness, Frank's declaration that he wishes to travel abroad, and soon, is tantamount to an expression of treason. 'I am sick of England,' he says, 'and would leave it to-morrow, if I could' (p. 330).

Emma offers him, as an alternative diversion, the expedition to Box Hill planned for the morrow: 'It is not Swisserland, but it will be something for a young man so much in want of a change.' Thus Box Hill, and the doomed pleasure party, is already, for the alert reader, marked as not truly 'English' — that is, it does not share the productivity and good order embodied in Donwell Abbey and farm. And if we have not noticed this not particularly subtle symbolism, Austen recaps it at the beginning of the Box Hill chapter:

> They had a very fine day for Box Hill; and all the other outward circumstances of arrangement, accommodation, and punctuality, were in favour of a pleasant party. ... Seven miles were travelled in

expectation of enjoyment, and everybody had a burst of admiration on first arriving; but in the general amount of the day there was deficiency. There was a languor, a want of spirits, a want of union, which could not be got over. They separated too much into parties. The Eltons walked together; Mr. Knightley took charge of Miss Bates and Jane; and Emma and Harriet belonged to Frank Churchill. And Mr. Weston tried, in vain, to make them harmonize better. It seemed at first an accidental division, but it never materially varied. Mr. and Mrs. Elton, indeed, showed no unwillingness to mix, and be as agreeable as they could; but during the two whole hours that were spent on the Hill, there seemed a principle of separation between the other parties, too strong for any fine prospects, or any cold collation, or any cheerful Mr. Weston, to remove. (pp. 331–2)

Box Hill *cannot* control socially disruptive influences, because it is merely a pleasure-place; its landscape does not imply and encourage those 'English' virtues so evident at Donwell. And it lacks the ordered structure of the Donwell landscape; while Emma has at various points in her past visited and admired Donwell, she 'had never been to Box Hill': to go there is to break bounds, to break out of the controlling habits of her life. It is no wonder that 'Mr Frank Churchill and Miss Woodhouse flirted together *excessively*.' Once again their language takes on, in another page of dialogue without speaker attributions, a theatrical quality: most notably, Frank's does, with declarations such as 'I saw you first in February. Let every body on the Hill hear me if they can. Let my accents swell to Mickleham on one side, and Dorking on the other. I saw you first in February.' Emma performs less wholeheartedly to begin with: 'she felt less happy than she had expected. She laughed because she was disappointed' (p. 333), and she is able at first to offer some sound observations based on the clearer judgement which Donwell encourages: 'you had, somehow or other, broken bounds yesterday, and run away from your own management; but today you are got back again'. What she cannot now be aware of is the depth of Frank's self-control, the game he is playing in earnest with both her and Jane. And under his stage management, it is Emma who will 'break bounds' today:

'Ladies and gentlemen, I am ordered by Miss Woodhouse (who, wherever she is, presides,) to say, that she desires to know what you are all thinking of.'
… Mr Knightley's answer was the most distinct.

'Is Miss Woodhouse sure that she would like to know what we are all thinking of?'
'Oh! no, no' — cried Emma, laughing as carelessly as she could — 'Upon no account in the world. It is the very last thing I would stand the brunt of just now ... ' (p. 334)

Frank is relentless in his pushing of Emma, who is already uncomfortable, beyond the bounds of social decorum: 'Ladies and gentlemen — I am ordered by Miss Woodhouse to say, that she waves her right of knowing exactly what you may all be thinking of, and only requires something very entertaining from each of you, in a general way ... ' (p. 335). Frank has played the role of hypnotic Svengali, or even the Tempter himself, to perfection: Emma finally 'could not resist' when humble Miss Bates offers herself as sacrifice. Emma's language now becomes totally and heartlessly theatrical — Miss Bates is confused by 'the mock ceremony of her manner' as Emma utters the insult: 'Ah! ma'am, but there may be a difficulty. Pardon me —but you will be limited as to number — only three at once.'

Only the insensitive good-humour of Mr Weston could possibly cap this; it is at this point that he offers his astonishingly inappropriate 'conundrum' on Emma's name. Being a hearty Englishman, he blunders in game-playing; he does not have the finesse of his cosmopolitan son. Nor does he have the moral weight of Mr Knightley, who 'gravely' makes a pun himself: '*Perfection* should not have come quite so soon.'

The game breaks up, its subversive aim (to make everyone feel as bad as Frank does himself) achieved, and the Eltons go off for a walk, Mrs Elton in passing once again demonstrating her linguistic incompetence: 'I am really tired of exploring so long on one spot.' This leaves the stage clear for Act Two of the Box Hill expedition: the 'double' dialogue between Frank and Jane which marks the crisis in their relationship. Frank begins it, thinking to insult Jane in terms that only she will recognise, as he is evidently referring to the circumstances of their first meeting. What *he* does not know is that he is contributing to the novelist's meta-game, the allegorising of *places* as representing certain spiritual qualities (as these two chapters' contrast of Donwell and Box Hill supremely demonstrates). He may think he is being cleverly insulting, but the second-time reader recognises that he is also expressing an important truth about relationships as the novel sees them:

'Happy couple!' said Frank Churchill, as soon as they were out of hearing; 'how well they suit one another! Very lucky — marrying as

31

they did, upon an acquaintance formed only in a public place! They only knew each other, I think, a few weeks in Bath! Peculiarly lucky! — for as to any real knowledge of a person's disposition that Bath, or any public place, can give — it is all nothing; there can be no knowledge. It is only by seeing women in their own homes, among their own set, just as they always are, that you can form any just judgment. Short of that, it is all guess and luck — and will generally be ill-luck. How many a man has committed himself on a short acquaintance, and rued it all the rest of his life!' (p. 337)

Jane's answer is a model of quiet moral strength, implicitly placing Frank among the 'weak, irresolute characters ... who will suffer an unfortunate acquaintance to be an inconvenience, an oppression for ever'. Frank understandably has 'no answer' to this, and turns his attention once again to Emma, intending to provoke Jane to jealousy by his request that Emma should 'choose a wife' for him. But it is perhaps his announcement that he will 'go abroad for a couple of years' that impels Jane to her final observation: ' "Now, ma'am," said Jane to her aunt, "shall we join Mrs Elton?" ' (p. 338) This too is a statement with double meaning: what has just occurred in this covert dialogue is the breaking-off of Jane and Frank's engagement, leaving Jane no alternative but to accede to the plans of Mrs Elton and take employment with the Sucklings and Bragges of this world.

The Box Hill picnic has a coda — not the Third Act of Frank's play, which we do not see in detail, only hearing that Frank's 'spirits now rose to a pitch almost unpleasant', but a private conversation between Emma and Mr Knightley (he makes sure, in contrast to Frank's exhibitionist behaviour, that it *is* private: 'He looked round, as if to see that no one were there ...' (p. 339)). His rebuke to Emma spells out what has been implicit in these two climactic chapters' consideration of the behaviour proper to the English gentry:

'Were she your equal in situation — but, Emma, consider how far this is from being the case. She is poor; she has sunk from the comforts she was born to; and if she live to old age must probably sink more. Her situation should secure your compassion. It was badly done, indeed! You, whom she had known from an infant, whom she had seen grow up from a period when her notice was an honour — to have you now, in thoughtless spirits, and the pride of the moment, laugh at her, humble her — and before her niece, too — and before others, many of whom (certainly *some*) would be entirely guided by *your* treatment of her.' (pp. 339–40)

Emma is 'forcibly struck' by 'the truth of his representation' — a phrase that could never apply to Frank Churchill's verbal performances — and 'felt it at her heart': Frank Churchill has never touched Emma's heart. Accordingly, she 'felt the tears running down her cheeks almost all the way home, without being at any trouble to check them, extraordinary as they were' (p. 341). The image suggests shame and penitence, and that Mr Knightley's role in the spiritual drama has been priest-like; further, we note (almost subliminally) that the effect of the 'excess' and disorder of the expedition to Box Hill has been to begin to melt the heart of the 'fair but frozen maid'.

The novel as allegory

I began this chapter by asking, 'Who *is* Frank Churchill?', and have argued that in the novel's allegory of good and evil he very clearly plays the role of Lucifer, the fair-seeming tempter of humanity's pride. In his general character of the charming young man, and his use of the modes of the theatre in order to control the behaviour of others, he is like Henry Crawford of Austen's immediately preceding novel, *Mansfield Park*. This is the novel in which 'home theatricals' literally play an important role, both in terms of the plot and in terms of the novel's consideration of good and evil. The two novels are more alike than many commentators have noticed — most strikingly so in the Frank and Emma-like characterisations of the energetic and brilliant Henry and Mary Crawford, but also in an authorial habit of naming which derives ultimately from the English Protestant tradition of allegory most famously embodied in John Bunyan's *Pilgrim's Progress* (1678). It does not take much thought to realise that Donwell Abbey is significantly named: it is the place in which good has been *done* for centuries (beginning in medieval times, under the aegis of the Church), and which Emma will finally make her home after she has 'done well' in her duty by her father. Most readers will have noticed the connotations of Mr Knightley's name: of the true old English gentry, 'untainted in blood and understanding', he chivalrously rescues Emma from her own worst enemy — herself. The fact that his first name is George is brought to our attention in the coy post-engagement dialogue between Emma and Mr Knightley, when she promises that she will at least once call him by his Christian name, 'in the building in which N. takes M. for better, for worse' (p. 420), that is, in the marriage service. The red-cross knight Saint George is of course the patron saint of England, of which, as we have already seen, Donwell Abbey is the epitome.

Although 'M. and A.' do not equal 'perfection' in the person of Emma herself, she too inhabits an allegorically named environment. 'Hartfield' is the field of struggle for the heart of the 'fair but frozen maid' (just as *Mansfield* is the field of struggle for the souls of the young adventurers in life that inhabit it — most notably, the virtuous heroine, Fanny Price); and despite its grand airs of being the residence of true gentry, it is, by comparison with Donwell, a 'wood house', its claims to moral authority hollow ('Woodhouse' is Emma's ineffectual *father's* name).

The minor characters are less significantly named, though we need to be told no more than their names tell us about Mrs Elton's fine friends the Sucklings and the Bragges. Frank Churchill and Jane Fairfax present a more subtle case of suggestive naming. Jane has her author's own Christian name, which might suggest a sympathetic identification between the novelist and the passionate and unhappy creature whose prospects for happiness are so remote. 'Fairfax', on the other hand, is the name of one of 'the original Causers of all the disturbances Distresses & Civil Wars in which England was for many years embroiled' ('The History of England', *Minor Works* , p. 148): Jane's breaking of the rules of social behaviour cannot be condoned. Frank is anything but frank, as we have seen, and the associations of piety and national honour in his surname Churchill (the family name of the great general the Duke of Marlborough in Queen Anne's reign) are specious: his true surname is of course Weston. Even more interestingly, the name *Frank* is cognate with *France* or *French*. Where John Churchill, Duke of Marlborough, was a great patriot, Frank is 'sick of England' and wishes to be out of it. Mr Knightley points out Frank's French affiliations even before we have met the man:

> '… No, Emma, your amiable young man can be amiable only in French, not in English. He may be very "aimable," have very good manners, and be very agreeable; but he can have no English delicacy towards the feelings of other people: nothing really amiable about him.' (pp. 134–5)

This notion of moral qualities embodied in a nation's language may well be a myth, but it is a powerful one which Jane Austen uses consistently throughout this text. Other examples occur in the narrator's own descriptive prose:

> John Knightley made his appearance, and 'How d'ye do, George?' and 'John, how are you?' succeeded in the true English style,

burying under a calmness that seemed all but indifference, the real attachment which would have led either of them, if requisite, to do every thing for the good of the other. (p. 90)

... in the judgment of most people looking on [Emma and Frank's behaviour] must have had such an appearance as no English word but flirtation could very well describe. (p. 332)

And when Mr Knightley asks Emma when they may marry, he does so 'in plain, unaffected, gentleman-like English, such as Mr Knightley used even to the woman he was in love with' (p. 407). English is plain and unpretentious; it is a language of 'truth and sincerity' (p. 404) and of the true hero Mr Knightley; French is the language associated with double-dealing, frivolity, and affectation, and the deceptively named Frank Churchill.

England was at war with Napoleonic France throughout Austen's adult life, and two of her brothers were engaged in active service in the Navy. She had good reason for her patriotic and conservative stance on what constituted true Englishness, and the need to defend it against cosmopolitan and *nouveau-riche* interlopers. The war against Napoleon had not been won when Austen was writing *Emma*: the threat of a French invasion was real.

In the novel it is the morally suspect characters, such as Frank or Mrs Elton, who generally use faddish French words which had only recently made their way into English usage. When Mr Knightley uses a French word, as in the example above, he does so in order to point out the moral and spiritual failings of the subject under discussion. Even the narrator observes this distinction. Some examples:

pic-nic (p. 318), imported into English 1748, and only to be associated with the vulgar Eltons and Sucklings and the activities of Maple Grove.

charade (Chapter 9 and others), imported into English 1776; a frivolous word-game which delights Harriet and appears to be the sum total of Mr Woodhouse's intellectual store.

manoeuvring and finessing (p. 132) — Mr Knightley's further condemnation of Frank Churchill's behaviour to his family. Much later, when all is made clear, Mr Knightley comments that Frank has been 'playing a most dangerous game ... his own mind full of *intrigue*, that he should suspect it in others. — Mystery; *Finesse* — how they pervert the understanding! ...' (p. 404). *Manoeuvre* is imported from French 1748 (as 'deceptive, elusive behaviour'; as a verb describing such behaviour its use dates from 1809).

Finessing as a verb dates from 1746. Emma considers Frank's secret engagement 'a system of hypocrisy and deceit, — *espionage*, and treachery' (p. 362): *espionage* only arrived in English in 1793, a word produced by the French Revolution.

Various French words had been part of fashionable English speech since the mid-seventeenth century. Mr Knightley never uses them, nor does the quiet Jane Fairfax, but Emma, Mr and Mrs Elton, and Frank — social exhibitionists all — do. Frank maliciously comments on Jane's hairdo at the Coles' party as *outrée* (p. 199). Harriet, to Emma's eyes early in the story, has 'a very interesting *naïeveté*' (p. 37), and Frank and Mr Elton also admire this quality in Harriet, implicitly contrasting it with their own sophistication. Emma wishes to 'avoid *éclat*' after her first disaster in managing Harriet's affairs of the heart (p. 124). When meeting Mrs Elton at the Bateses' after the announcement of Jane's engagement, 'she hoped the *rencontre* would do them no harm' (p. 411) — a word which previously occurs in Emma's fantasy arising from Harriet's encounter with the gipsies, and Mr Elton's account of his speedy courtship of the lovely Augusta Hawkins (p. 162). This lady flaunts the Sucklings' possession of a *barouche landau* three times in one paragraph (p. 246) (this elaborate carriage was invented in 1804), preferring it to their *chaise*, whereas the inhabitants of Highbury use simple 'carriages'. Mrs Elton wishes to have *carte-blanche* (p. 320) in organising the Donwell strawberry party, and sees herself as *Chaperon* of the Box Hill party (p. 334).

The novel subtly operates an allegorical pattern in which England and Englishness (including speech itself, 'plain, unaffected, gentleman-like English', p. 407) is a vessel of moral and spiritual virtue, with a well-defined enemy in the devious characteristics of the nation across the Channel. If their language has already successfully invaded that of the English gentry, is it not dangerously possible that their morals and their revolutionary politics might do so as well?

WHY MARRY?

Although wishing to organise all the eligible single people in her environs (always excepting Mr Knightley, of course) into marriage, Emma herself declares early in the novel, in conversation with the astonished Harriet,

> 'I cannot really change for the better. If I were to marry, I must expect to repent it.'
> 'Dear me! it is so odd to hear a woman talk so!'

It is indeed; it was close to revolutionary in Jane Austen's day. And yet what Emma says, and goes on to say, is experientially verifiable truth:

> 'I have none of the usual inducements of women to marry. ... without love, I am sure I should be a fool to change such a situation as mine. Fortune I do not want; employment I do not want; consequence I do not want; I believe few married women are half as much mistress of their husband's house as I am of Hartfield; and never, never could I expect to be so truly beloved and important; so always first and always right in any man's eyes as I am in my father's.' (p. 77)

Emma was not the only early-nineteenth-century woman who preferred the safety of a known and comfortable domestic situation to the possible perils of the married state. Jane Austen herself turned down several serious suitors and, like her creation, preferred to imagine the love lives of others rather than set sail on the often stormy seas of love herself. Emma, when wondering if she is in love with Frank Churchill, finds in her fantasies that she always '*refused him*' (p. 237).

Harriet's worry that Emma will end up with the stigma of being 'an old maid at last, like Miss Bates' is treated to a cool political analysis by Emma:

> 'Never mind, Harriet, I shall not be a poor old maid; and it is poverty only which makes celibacy contemptible to a generous public! A single woman, with a very narrow income must be a ridiculous, disagreeable old maid! the proper sport of boys and girls; but a single woman, of good fortune, is always respectable, and may be as sensible and pleasant as anybody else. And the distinction is not quite so much against the candour and common sense of the world as appears at first; for a very narrow income has a tendency to contract the mind, and sour the temper. Those who can barely live, and who live perforce in a very small, and generally very inferior, society, may well be illiberal and cross.' (p. 77)

Desire

Generations of critics, especially since Marvin Mudrick's radical rereading, *Jane Austen:Irony as Defense and Discovery* (1952), have been disturbed by Emma's apparent coldness to 'normal' sexual feeling. She is often accused of being in love unconsciously with Harriet;[1] but this is to ignore Austen's sophisticated play with conventions of contemporary literature — the romance in particular (see above, p. 14) — in favour of twentieth-century Freudian critical readings which use the text as an exposure of hidden motives in the characters or the author. Mudrick's amateur psychoanalysis is based on naive assumptions about the 'reality' of fictional characters: 'Harriet begins to seem a kind of proxy for Emma, a means by which Emma — too reluctant, too fearful of involvement, to consider the attempt herself — may discover what marriage is like.' (Mudrick, in Lodge, p. 126) Even using the criteria of realism, can we imagine Emma asking Harriet 'What's it like?' and getting a coherent answer? And why would Emma not ask her ex-governess for further information on the 'facts of life' if she wanted them? Or her sister? It is surely no coincidence that the critics thus affronted are almost invariably male: is Emma refusing the place allotted her gender in a patriarchal society? Is she thus refusing to play her part in *their* romance? We might perhaps more accurately say that *Austen* is in love with Emma ('a heroine whom no one but myself will much like') as an image of the 'authoring' personality, that is, of her own powers; but that would provide a considerably more sophisticated picture of the author's control of her text than the psychoanalytic critics would allow.

Claudia Johnson, one of the new generation of scholarly feminist critics, argues that

> the guarantor of order [Mr Knightley] himself cedes a considerable portion of the power which custom has allowed him to expect. In moving to Hartfield, Knightley is sharing *her* home, and in placing himself within her domain, Knightley gives his blessing to her rule.
> ... eccentricity is one of the privileges of the elite, and in this case it permits the hero and heroine to be husband and wife, yet live and rule together with the autonomy of friends. (p. 143)

'I love to look at her,' comments Mr Knightley in that early, establishing conversation between himself and Mrs Weston about Emma's radiant good health and 'loveliness' (p. 34). And lest we have missed this clue, and that provided by the first chapter's information that he was 'a frequent visitor' (p. 7 — what, after all, can attract him to Hartfield but Emma's presence? Certainly not the conversation of Mr Woodhouse), we have the ongoing evidence that Emma and Mr Knightley enjoy each other's company. There is an undercurrent of familiar flirtation (so familar as to be unrecognised) in almost all their recorded conversations, as well as the tutelary role which readers tend to remember because of the climactic moment of Mr Knightley's rebuke over Emma's rudeness to Miss Bates. But this sort of exchange is more typical of their talk: 'Mr Knightley loves to find fault with me you know — in a joke — it is all a joke. We always say what we like to one another' (p. 8); 'Nonsensical girl!' (p. 192). It is also made clear to the watchful reader that Mr Knightley is jealous of Frank Churchill, the apparently more eligible suitor. Austen places the crucial conversation at the end of Volume One of the book's original format: their long and heated discussion of the personal qualities of the as yet unseen Frank Churchill (this is the conversation in which Mr Knightley displays his linguistic patriotism in the discussion of Frank's 'amiability'). Mr Knightley gets less and less like his usual calm self as Emma persists in elaborating on her fantasies about Frank ('My idea of him is, that he can adapt his conversation to the taste of every body, and has the power

39

as well as the wish of being universally agreeable', p. 135); and the recorded conversation — and the volume — concludes with:

> 'He is a person I never think of from one month's end to another,' said Mr Knightley, with a degree of vexation, which made Emma immediately talk of something else, though she could not comprehend why he should be angry. (p. 136)

There follows a short paragraph of reflection by Emma on 'the real liberality of mind which she was always used to acknowledge' in Mr Knightley, and her surprise that in this one case of Frank Churchill it seems not to be operating. Even the first-time reader should be able to pick up the hint offered by Austen here, and make the obvious deduction that Emma cannot recognise Mr Knightley's very understandable jealousy. Nor, perhaps, can Mr Knightley. For Frank irrupts into Volume Two as first and foremost a sexual being, young, handsome, and charming; a player who uses parlour-games and other frivolous occupations of the gentry as a sort of currency in the recognised mode of flirtation. Mr Knightley's arrival at Hartfield in Chapter 1, we remember, made the backgammon table 'unnecessary'. Neither a game-player, and 'no dancer in general' (p. 207), in the sexually sleepy world of Highbury Mr Knightley has had no occasion to display his sexuality, sublimating it rather into social paternalism in the day-to-day business of the concerned landholder. Emma is instinctively right in her teasing him about the importance of the offstage William Larkins, his estate manager. When the Crown ball is first proposed, Mr Knightley grumpily claims that he 'would rather be at home, looking over William Larkins's week's account' (p. 231); when it is cancelled Emma thinks 'Mr Knightley will be happy. He may spend the evening with his dear William Larkins now if he likes' (p. 236). And when it comes to the difficulty over Emma's refusal to leave her father or Hartfield in order to marry, it is Mr Knightley who gives in:

> He had given it, he could assure her, very long and calm consideration; he had been walking away from William Larkins the whole morning to have his thoughts to himself.
>   'Ah! there is one difficulty unprovided for,' cried Emma. 'I am sure William Larkins will not like it. You must get his consent before you ask mine.' (p. 408)

If we do (with caution) use the Freudian model and see Emma's interest in Harriet as a displacement of her own sexual energy, we must read Mr Knightley and William Larkins in the same light, as structural parallels. Austen's point is presumably that at the highest level of its social hierarchy, Highbury has become desexualised. After all, Mr Woodhouse is, after Mr Knightley, the chief gentleman of the place, and he seems even to have forgotten the facts of life: 'they did see [Mr Knightley] every day as it was. — Why could not they go on as they had done?' (p. 424). Highbury needs revitalising from within, by realising its own sexual potential.

The Crown ball fulfils the underlying purpose of all dancing — that is, of being a mating ritual, by showing off the community's young people in their finest plumage. And, most specifically, it is the occasion for Mr Knightley to be seen as an eligible male — as he is by Emma, in a revealing passage of reflection:

> She was was more disturbed by Mr Knightley's not dancing, than by anything else. There he was, among the standers-by, where he ought not to be; he ought to be dancing, not classing himself with the husbands, and fathers, and whist-players, who were pretending to feel an interest in the dance till their rubbers were made up, so young as he looked! He could not have appeared to greater advantage perhaps anywhere, than where he had placed himself. His tall, firm, upright figure, among the bulky forms and stooping shoulders of the elderly men, was such as Emma felt must draw every body's eyes; and, excepting her own partner, there was not one among the whole row of young men who could be compared with him. He moved a few steps nearer, and those few steps were enough to prove in how gentlemanlike a manner, with what natural grace, he must have danced, would he but take the trouble. (p. 293)

'His tall, firm, upright figure' — the image of potent masculinity — 'was such as Emma felt must draw every body's eyes': oddly enough, it seems only to draw Emma's. She is here very close to recognising her own attraction to Mr Knightley, and by the end of the chapter her body, at any rate, has expressed its desire. She has, after a moment of hesitation, asked him to dance with her (she has already with 'her eyes invited him irresistibly to come to her and be thanked' for rescuing Harriet from Mr Elton's snub, p. 297). But she is not yet ready to hear what her heart and body know, and passes off her desire to dance with him with the flippant and perhaps slightly uncomfortable comment, 'we are not really so much brother and sister as to make it at all improper'. 'Brother and sister! no, indeed,' replies Mr Knightley, leaving their

conversation while they dance to the imagination of the reader as
Austen teasingly ends the chapter.

A comparable moment of body language occurs at the moment of
their reconciliation after the Box Hill rebuke:

> He looked at her with a glow of regard. She was warmly gratified —
> and in another moment still more so, by a little movement of more
> than common friendliness on his part. He took her hand; whether
> she had not herself made the first motion, she could not say — she
> might, perhaps, have rather offered it — but he took her hand,
> pressed it, and certainly was on the point of carrying it to his lips —
> when, from some fancy or other, he suddenly let it go. Why he
> should feel such a scruple, why he should change his mind when it
> was all but done, she could not perceive. He would have judged
> better, she thought, if he had not stopped. (p. 349)

Austen's favourite words[2] when talking about the current of attraction between bodies, *glow*, *warmly*, here alert us to a moment when the
body's desires briefly control the actions of these two rational people:
'He took her hand; whether she had not herself made the first motion,
she could not say — she might, perhaps, have rather offered it'. It is of
course Mr Knightley's jealousy of Frank which leads him to interrupt
the potential kiss, and Emma regrets what she has missed: 'He would
have judged better, she thought, if he had not stopped.'

Jane Austen most famously teases the reader in the 'love scene'
between Emma and Mr Knightley, the moment when all this sup-
pressed love and desire is finally spoken of. Emma has realised, only
two days previously, that she is indeed the victim of Cupid's dart: 'it
darted through her, with the speed of an arrow, that Mr Knightley
must marry no one but herself!' (p. 370). But she quite quickly per-
suades herself that Harriet's 'romance' with him is not unlikely — 'Was
it a new circumstance for a man of first-rate abilites to be captivated by
very inferior powers? Was it new for one, perhaps too busy to seek, to
be the prize of a girl who would seek him?' (p. 375); and that

> Marriage, in fact, would not do for her. It would be incompatible
> with what she owed to her father, and with what she felt for him.
> Nothing should separate her from her father. She would not marry,
> even if she were asked by Mr. Knightley. (p. 377)

Emma's self-deception is a habit that is hard to break; and what has
always been problematic in it is that she acts as though her fictions were
true, thus embroidering them and complicating their effects. In this

case, Mr Knightley returns from London and comes to walk with Emma in her garden. The weather has improved, 'it was summer again'; the stage is obviously set for a love scene, but Emma is determined to play it as a scene between neutral friends:

> Mr. Knightley startled her by saying:
> 'You will not ask me what is the point of envy. You are determined, I see, to have no curiosity. You are wise — but I cannot be wise. Emma, I must tell what you will not ask, though I may wish it unsaid the next moment.'
> 'Oh! then, don't speak it, don't speak it,' she eagerly cried. 'Take a little time, consider, do not commit yourself.'
> 'Thank you,' said he, in an accent of deep mortification, and not another syllable followed. (p. 389)

The comic misunderstandings and awkwardness continue just as they so often do in real life, on the parts of both characters in this momentous scene:

> 'My dearest Emma,' said he, 'for dearest you will always be, whatever the event of this hour's conversation, my dearest, most beloved Emma — tell me at once. Say "No," if it is to be said.' She could really say nothing. 'You are silent,' he cried, with great animation; 'absolutely silent! at present I ask no more.'
> Emma was almost ready to sink under the agitation of this moment. (p. 390)

And while Mr Knightley speaks his love, Emma's thoughts are mingled with Jane Austen's ironical perspective to give us the anti-climactic climax to this anti-romantic love scene:

> as to any of that heroism of sentiment which might have prompted her to entreat him to transfer his affection from herself to Harriet, as infinitely the most worthy of the two — or even the more simple sublimity of resolving to refuse him at once and for ever, without vouchsafing any motive because he could not marry them both, Emma had it not. She felt for Harriet, with pain and with contrition; but no flight of generosity run mad, opposing all that could be probable or reasonable, entered her brain. ... What did she say? — Just what she ought, of course. A lady always does. (p. 391)

Austen deliberately distances the reader at this crucial point from any soft-focus romantic fantasy. She does it by two major techniques: first, by a vocabulary which reminds us of the conventions of contemporary sentimental fiction, what we might normally expect in a novel of this period: *heroism of sentiment, simple sublimity of resolving to refuse him* — note here the gushing alliteration, then the hyperbolic adverbial phrase *at once and for ever*. To this is opposed the *probable or reasonable* — the emotionally realistic world of Austen's fictional concerns. And when, in that famous and teasing narratorial evasion, Austen remarks, 'Just what she ought, of course. A lady always does', she is not only protecting the privacy of her heroine and hero (as she invariably does in all her novels), she is also, by her ironic and defensive tone, reminding us forcefully of the social dimension of her novel. If asked to summarise the concerns of *Emma*, we might well answer: what it means to be a *lady*, especially the 'first lady' of Highbury, or any community; what is the appropriate behaviour for a lady; what Emma has to learn in order to graduate into being 'Mrs Knightley' of Donwell Abbey. Austen is here acknowledging the limitations of the social world and its hierarchy that she has been at pains to present as potentially ideal (the view from Donwell Abbey). These limitations are suggested elsewhere in the novel, as a counterpoint to Emma's story: in the less-fortunate stories of Jane Fairfax and her indigent gentlewoman aunt Miss Bates; and in the figure of Mrs Elton, the woman of doubtful family who does *not* know how to behave like a lady, although she knows all the outward forms that are due to her.

Emma complains during the Woodhouse family discussion about the virtues of various bathing places for the health that *she* has 'never seen the sea' (p. 91). On her honeymoon with Mr Knightley, a 'tour to the sea-side' (p. 439), she will at last see it, and we may read this as a final example of Austen's allegory of place in this novel. For the sea is a symbol of wild feeling, uncontained emotion: it is the quintessential romantic image, and as such is used extensively by Jane Austen in the next novel she was to write, *Persuasion*, where Byron's famous lyric 'Roll on, thou deep and dark blue ocean — roll!' is the subject of conversation between the heroine Anne and the melancholic Captain Benwick (*Persuasion*, p. 106) as they contemplate the seascape at Lyme. Anne, of course, marries a sailor, who has many of the virtues of the admirable Mr Knightley, but with a touch of romantic mystery and passion; she herself knows that she is passionately in love from the moment of their meeting again after their long separation. *Persuasion* is in many ways Austen's most romantic novel; certainly that in which she offers the most sympathetic exploration of passionate feeling in the heroine. Emma's honeymoon at the seaside is, I think, Jane Austen's way of letting us know subliminally that she will experience with Mr Knightley something she has never yet known — passionate sexual love. Before the wedding Emma imagines that she can never call him 'George' — but there are obviously limits to her potential as an 'imaginist', worlds of experience that she has not dreamt of in the cosy toytown of Highbury.

Jane's situation

Jane Fairfax is in every respect Emma's social equal, except that she has no money and no prospects of inheritance. She is in fact more 'accomplished' than Emma, being a better pianist and having more educated taste: in fact, she has had advantages that Emma has not: 'Col. Campbell's residence being in London, every lighter talent had been done full justice to, by the attendance of first-rate masters' (p. 146). Emma, we remember, has had the easy authority of Miss Taylor for her education, and she herself regrets that she had not practised more, read more and improved on her artistic talents.

Jane's lack of money is the principal fact of her situation, however. At twenty-one (the same age as Emma), she has determined no longer to be a burden on her friends the Campbells, but to 'enter on her path of duty' (p. 147) and seek work as a governess. The effect of this will be to reduce her social status from that of 'lady' to that of 'gentlewoman', one who must engage in some form of remunerated labour in the household of well-off gentry. Jane herself, in the bitterness of wondering if her secret engagement to Frank will ever be fulfilled, speaks of 'places in town, offices, where inquiry would soon produce something — Offices for the sale — not quite of human flesh — but of human intellect' (p. 271). She will be extraordinarily lucky if, like Miss Taylor, in this situation she meets some man who is happy to marry her and reintroduce her to 'equal society'. Emma represents the novel's feminist awareness on this matter: 'the contrast between Mrs Churchill's importance in the world, and Jane Fairfax's, struck her; one was every thing, the other nothing–and she sat musing on the difference of woman's destiny' (p. 348).

In this novel's symbolic scheme, only Jane's passionate involvement with Frank can save her from the situation of 'penance and mortification for ever' (p. 147) — no amiable and honourable Mr Dixon offers himself. Is it worth it? the novel seems to ask. Is it worth denying so many of one's principles of right behaviour in order to pursue the faint hope offered by Frank of passional fulfilment and social status? The second-time reader is witness to what veritably becomes the torture of Jane Fairfax as Frank forces her to play his game — 'So cold and artificial! I had always a part to act. It was a life of deceit!' (p. 418) — which she herself castigates as 'very great misconduct' (p. 417). At first his audacity gives her pleasure: the piano is a physical manifestation of his love; Emma suspects that 'she had not yet possessed the instrument long enough to touch it without emotion' (p. 216), though the object of that emotion is wrongly identified. Frank is evidently hugely pleased with himself over the gift, and speaks with a gleeful ambiguity which arouses 'a smile of secret delight' in Jane (pp. 218–19). But in Chapter 41 — one of the rare moments when the point of view moves away from Emma — Mr Knightley observes the actions of Frank in the alphabet-game as he covertly sends messages to Jane: 'It was a child's play,' thinks Mr Knightley, 'chosen to conceal a deeper game on Frank Churchill's part' (p. 314). He then observes the way Emma is drawn with small protest into the game of teasing Jane:

> It was done, however. This gallant young man, who seemed to love without feeling, and to recommend himself without complaisance, directly handed over the word to Miss Fairfax, and with a particular degree of sedate civility entreated her to study it. Mr. Knightley's excessive curiosity to know what this word might be, made him seize every possible moment for darting his eye towards it, and it was not long before he saw it to be *Dixon*. Jane Fairfax's perception seemed to accompany his; her comprehension was certainly more equal to the covert meaning, the superior intelligence, of those five letters so arranged. She was evidently displeased; looked up, and seeing herself watched, blushed more deeply than he had ever perceived her, and saying only, 'I did not know that proper names were allowed,' pushed away the letters with even an angry spirit, and looked resolved to be engaged by no other word that could be offered. Her face was averted from those who had made the attack, and turned towards her aunt. (pp. 314–15)

Embarrassment and anger at an unwarranted attack on her ethics, in addition to the continual distress of seeing Frank flirt more and more outrageously with Emma, are a lead-up to the dual crisis in their relationship precipitated by the Donwell and Box Hill expeditions. The fact that Frank is momentarily sorry for his misbehaviour (according to Austen family tradition, the final word that Frank 'anxiously pushed towards her', and that she as 'resolutely pushed away' was *pardon*) is no brake on his game-playing activities, as we see in the two following chapters. They are a dangerous relief for the sexual and emotional tension of the unfulfilled relationship, and Jane, finally, has had enough. She breaks off the engagement, but (because it is not a public declaration) this does not improve her emotional state. In fact, she becomes ill as a result of the total loss of hope in her life. The extreme action of her walking home from Donwell in the heat of the day is a precursor of the image of her 'wandering about the meadows' (p. 354) like the forsaken girls of Gothic novels, driven mad by being jilted by their lovers. She is refusing food (including Emma's anxious offering of 'very superior' arrowroot), 'suffering under severe headachs, and a nervous fever to a degree, which made [Mr Perry] doubt the possibility of her going to Mrs Smallridge's at the time proposed. Her health seemed for the moment completely deranged . . .' (p. 353). Jane's is the tragic flip-side of Emma's comic story: what can happen to a woman without means of support if she relies only on passionate sexual love to give her life meaning. A further tradition in Austen's family had it that Jane did not long survive the marriage.

FINAL MANOEUVRES

Jane Fairfax, the heroine of the 'hidden narrative' in the novel, is literally a 'displaced' person: parentless, living on the charity of friends and poor relations. Is Highbury her home, or London, or will she be condemned to make a home for limited periods wherever employment offers itself? In this mobility she is like Frank, who lives sometimes in Yorkshire, sometimes in London, Richmond or Windsor, and who met Jane at the fashionable watering-place Weymouth. It looks as though, as the novel draws to its close, Jane is going to be obliged to enter the world of realistic economic facts, rather than have fulfilled the romantic fantasy of marriage to a handsome and rich young man. But Austen as comic puppet-mistress has the last laugh on readers who might be inclined to moralise here: if Jane and Frank are the romantic and passionate lovers they of course must be united according to the rules of their own fictional world. Death and inheritance, happening unexpectedly offstage, free them to marry; though the reader, who sees them together only in Highbury, may well wonder what their mode of life will be once the thrill of secrecy no longer feeds their romance (their final scene together in the novel is perhaps indicative: see discussion below, p. 54).

Meanwhile, Mr Knightley has had to leave Highbury and the comfort of conversation with William Larkins in order to deal with his own emotional distress in believing he had lost Emma after her excessive flirtation with Frank Churchill at Box Hill. This has symbolic as well as psychological aptness: if he has never gone further beyond Highbury than the market town of Kingston, then as a 'hero' he will look provincial and timid compared with the dashing Frank (who thinks nothing of riding sixteen miles to London for a decent haircut — or a piano). But Mr Knightley can also, at need, rise to a romantic gesture: 'He had ridden home through the rain' (p. 393) as soon as he heard that Emma was free of any tie to Frank.

Mr Knightley's experience of London is not of the huge anonymous city, but of his brother's house in Brunswick Square, a newish but unfashionable area at this time. As Isabella says, her brainless prattle acting as a conduit for Austen's symbolism,

> 'No, indeed — we are not at all in a bad air. Our part of London is so very superior to most others! — You must not confound us with London in general, my dear sir. The neighbourhood of Brunswick Square is very different from almost all the rest. We are so very airy!'
> (p. 93)

Consequently, Mr Knightley finds that

> he had gone to a wrong place [to forget Emma]. There was too much domestic happiness in his brother's house; woman wore too amiable a form in it; Isabella was too much like Emma — differing only in those striking inferiorities, which always brought the other in brilliancy before him. (p. 392)

As this suggests, John Knightley's living in London does carry a certain spiritual critique within the book's allegorical pattern. From what we see of his marriage, he is making the best of a not very brilliant situation. His wife is silly and hypochondriacal, and he himself is noticeably short-tempered. He is the sort of man, presumably, like Mr Bennet, who was 'captivated by youth and beauty, and that appearance of good humour, which youth and beauty generally give' (*Pride and Prejudice*, p. 209), rather than undertaking the long and almost imperceptible courtship of familiarity which Emma and Mr Knightley engage in, and which the novel clearly presents as preferable to the courtship styles of the other couples: Jane and Frank, and Mr Elton and Augusta Hawkins. The Westons, of course, correspond to the Knightley–Emma model of familiarity, and it has a particular symbolic resonance that their child is born during the course of the novel: little Anna is a harbinger of Highbury's revitalised fertility — the effect that

Mr Knightley's move to Hartfield will have in replacing the effete patriarch Mr Woodhouse with the 'firm and upright figure' of a man who fulfils his proper role in the community. The fact that we do not see Emma translated in triumph to Donwell is of crucial importance to Austen's project in this novel. In *Sense and Sensibility* (1811) we are offered a final image of the two sisters living in 'constant communication' between their husbands' houses at Barton and Delaford; in *Pride and Prejudice* (1813) we are invited to contemplate Elizabeth and Darcy happily ensconced in the great estate of Pemberley, surrounded by those they love best; in *Mansfield Park* (1814), the novel immediately preceding *Emma*, we see Fanny and Edmund, 'the married cousins', happy inhabitants of the parsonage, 'within the view and patronage of Mansfield Park'. But Mr Knightley, the owner of a property which is even more symbolically loaded with spiritual significance than Pemberley, Donwell Abbey, chooses to make the ultimate sacrifice for love and move to Hartfield while Emma's father lives.

As well as being a powerful symbol of Mr Knightley's genuine care for the community to which he belongs, this plot-move has significance in terms of the kind of novel Austen is writing, and its ongoing critique of romance (which always opts for the 'perfect' ending for its young lovers). As we have seen, Mr Knightley and Emma are not the usual types of romantic lovers — there is sixteen years' age difference between them, and Mr Knightley has known Emma since she was a baby. Moreover, they have lived in the same little community all their lives; there is nothing exotic in their knowing each other. Austen builds on this basic *donnée* in the way she structures her story's end: romance is dismissed, or at least subverted, and something much more closely resembling reality takes its place. That this is *not* 'reality', but a clever artist's imitation for her own ends — to discredit romance — is something which it is the chief task of Austen's verbal irony to convey to us, once the 'hidden' plot has been revealed and all emotional misunderstandings sorted out.

The novel's last two chapters play the old game of tying up loose ends, but they do so in so subtle a way that we hardly notice this is being done. First of all, the case of Harriet Smith must be resolved. The romance mode dictates that she should meet again her true love, Robert Martin, from whom she has been cruelly separated by the twists of fate or the tyranny of those more powerful than she. This is the pattern that Austen burlesques in *Northanger Abbey* when Henry

Tilney arrives out of the blue at the disconsolate heroine's home, having ridden across two counties when he learned of his father's discourteous behaviour to her. In *Emma* the reunion happens offstage, in the sophisticated city of London to which both 'hero' and 'heroine' of Harriet's romance have been sent by the agency of their social superiors Mr Knightley and Emma (Emma having spent most of the novel tyrannically blocking Harriet's love affair with Robert). And it happens in a completely mundane and ordinary social fashion, as Robert is invited to join the John Knightley family (which Harriet is visiting) on a visit to Astley's circus. We are told about it, however, via a conversation between Emma and Mr Knightley, now acknowledged lovers but still striking exactly the same familiar note in their conversations as they have done since the novel's first chapter:

> 'You ought to know your friend best … but I should say she was a good-tempered, soft-hearted girl, not likely to be very, very determined against any young man who told her he loved her.'
> Emma could not help laughing as she answered, 'Upon my word, I believe you know her quite as well as I do. But, Mr Knightley, are you perfectly sure that she has absolutely and downright accepted him? I could suppose she might in time, but can she already? Did not you misunderstand him? You were both talking of other things; of business, shows of cattle, or new drills; and might not you, in the confusion of so many subjects, mistake him? It was not Harriet's hand that he was certain of — it was the dimensions of some famous ox.'
> … 'Do you dare say this?' cried Mr Knightley. 'Do you dare to suppose me so great a blockhead as not to know what a man is talking of? What do you deserve?'
> 'Oh! I always deserve the best treatment, because I never put up with any other; and, therefore, you must give me a plain, direct answer. Are you quite sure that you understand the terms on which Mr Martin and Harriet now are?'
> 'I am quite sure,' he replied, speaking very distinctly. (p. 430)

The familiar repartee of this exchange buffers readers from any incredulity they may feel at the neatness of this resolution, at the same time as it burlesques that very neatness (it is more *likely* that Mr Knightley and Robert Martin were speaking of farming matters). Emma, in reflection after this news has been imparted, becomes herself almost an embodiment of the spirit of comedy which rules the novel's construction despite its serious moral:

She was in dancing, singing, exclaiming spirits; and till she had moved about, and talked to herself, and laughed and reflected, she could be fit for nothing rational.

... Serious she was, very serious, in her thankfulness and in her resolutions; and yet there was no preventing a laugh, sometimes in the very midst of them. She must laugh at such a close — such an end of the doleful disappointment of five weeks back — such a heart — such a Harriet! (pp. 431–2)

For the final meeting between Emma and Frank Churchill, with Jane in the same room as his acknowledged fiancée, Austen returns to the mode of dramatic dialogue which is the common currency of conversation between Frank and Emma. But now their game-playing tendency is one of the actual subjects of their conversation:

'... what an impudent dog I was! how could I dare — '
But he laughed so heartily at the recollection that Emma could not help saying:
'I do suspect that in the midst of your perplexities at that time, you had very great amusement in tricking us all. I am sure you had. I am sure it was a consolation to you.'
'Oh, no, no, no! how can you suspect me of such a thing? I was the most miserable wretch.'
'Not quite so miserable as to be insensible to mirth. I am sure it was a source of high entertainment to you, to feel that you were taking us all in. Perhaps I am the readier to suspect, because, to tell you the truth, I think it might have been some amusement to myself in the same situation. I think there is a little likeness between us.'
He bowed. (p. 435)

The bow is a theatrical gesture, one never used by Mr Knightley (he shakes hands in greeting). Five out of the six 'bows' in the novel are the actions of Frank Churchill: 'liberal allowances were made for the little excesses of such a handsome young man — one who smiled so often and bowed so well' (p. 185). The only other one is the would-be gallant Mr Elton: both gentlemen are playing at courtship, and courtesy, for their own advantage.

The other subject of Frank and Emma's conversation at this meeting is Jane herself, also present in the room. This is the last occasion on which the reader will observe Jane Fairfax, and Austen uses it to underline her role of tragic heroine in the novel's 'alternative story' — the one Jane Austen chose not to write, by concentrating on Emma's situation rather than Jane's. Frank's effusions on Jane's beauty serve to remind us of her physical type — the exact opposite of the 'picture of health' Emma. Jane's 'delicate' complexion combined with dark eyelashes and hair mark her as a figure in a potential tragic or at least serious drama of high life: Frank emphasises this by drawing our attention to her unconsciously theatrical pose:

'... She is a complete angel. Look at her. Is not she an angel in every gesture? Observe the turn of her throat. Observe her eyes, as she is looking up at my father. — You will be glad to hear (inclining his head, and whispering seriously) that my uncle means to give her all my aunt's jewels. They are to be new set. I am resolved to have some in an ornament for the head. Will not it be beautiful in her dark hair?' (p. 435)

What we also observe here is that Jane is condemned to exist in a world in which she is primarily an object, a possession, to be decorated and shown off by the triumphant male (notice 'an ornament for *the* head'). The tone of Frank's praise of his prize here is very different from the bluff frankness of Mr Knightley's 'I love to look at her' in response to Mrs Weston's early comments on Emma's blooming good health. His down-to-earth, familar love will never lead him to call Emma an 'angel', nor to emulate the sort of sadistic game-playing which next minute has Frank referring gleefully in public to the trials of their secret courtship. Jane's last words in the novel are hardly promising for the continuing happiness of their relationship:

Jane was forced to smile completely for a moment; and the smile partly remained as she turned towards him, and said, in a conscious, low, yet steady voice,
    'How you can bear such recollections is astonishing to me. They *will* sometimes obtrude; but how you can *court* them!' (p. 436)

The reader is pleased to know that 'Emma's feelings were chiefly with Jane' as Frank attempts to override this serious note with banter — we don't hear him, and nor, really, does Emma: he has no power over her now, as she contemplates instead the 'high superiority of character' of her own affianced lover.

Since Harriet, 'the natural daughter of somebody' (p. 19), was cast by Emma as the heroine of a romance, it is only fair to her and to the readers of her story that the mystery about her birth be cleared up as it always is in romance, generally to the social advantage of the heroine.

And, unsurprisingly in Austen's anti-romance, she turns out to be not of aristocratic origin but 'the daughter of a tradesman'. Here Austen's politics again seem to be foregrounded (as they were in the encomium on 'Englishness' at Donwell Abbey): although this passage is in Emma's 'voice', it is difficult to read it ironically when it opens with the following commonsense observation (which with *untainted* echoes the Donwell passage):

> It was likely to be as untainted, perhaps, as the blood of many a gentleman: but what a connexion had she been preparing for Mr Knightley–or for the Churchills–or even for Mr Elton! — The stain of illegitimacy, unbleached by nobility or wealth, would have been a stain indeed. (p. 438)

Harriet instead is firmly established in the world of everyday reality, to be nurtured by an ideology of good sense signalled by Austen's use of sentences with a symmetry which echoes the style of her favourite moralist Dr Johnson:

> She would be placed in the midst of those who loved her, and who had better sense than herself; retired enough for safety, and occupied enough for cheerfulness. She would be never led into temptation, nor left for it to find her out. She would be respectable and happy… (p. 438)

The novel ends, however, as it began, with comic irony foregrounded as we are told the story of the nuptials of Emma and Mr Knightley. 'Mr Woodhouse — how was Mr Woodhouse to be induced to consent?' is the final problem to be overcome by the hero and heroine of this anti-romance. Just like the protagonists of romances and fairytales, they are provided by the storyteller with a helper, a marvellous event: 'In this state of suspense they were befriended, not by any sudden illumination of Mr Woodhouse's mind, or any wonderful change in his nervous system,' — that *would* be a miracle! — 'but by the operation of the same system in another way'. That is, the unexpected change in the lovers' fortune is brought about by a realistic disturbance of the normal peaceable order of Highbury. 'Mrs Weston's poultry-house was robbed one night of all her turkies — evidently by the ingenuity of man' (I like to think of this as the gipsies' revenge, a reminder to Austen's possibly complacent conservative audience that prosperity and peace did not reign in all classes of British society at this time). 'Pilfering' — a deliberately trivialising word — 'was *housebreaking* to

Mr Woodhouse's fears'. Mr Woodhouse may well neurotically fear this trivial event, for there is a subliminal suggestion in the novel's punning nomenclature that he himself is the emotional equivalent of a wooden poultry-house, certainly not the embodiment of all that's best in English masculinity, as Mr Knightley of Donwell Abbey is. An attack on a poultry-house is therefore psychologically an attack on Mr Woodhouse himself. However, the knightly virtues, 'strength, resolution, and presence of mind ... commanded his fullest dependence. While either of them [George and John Knightley] protected him and his, Hartfield was safe'. Mr Woodhouse is a fully 'feminised' figure; his paternal and patriarchal authority is ceded to a figure who truly deserves to hold it, one who has demonstrated his *moral* authority throughout the narrative.

So as the novel draws to a close Austen deploys both her allegorising and moralising mode *and* the comic irony which undercuts the potential self-righteousness of such a practice. The union of Emma and Mr Knightley, with all that that symbolises, can come about because Mr Woodhouse is frightened of chicken-thieves. For a similar artistic reason, the egregiously vulgar Mrs Elton invades the novel's final paragraph: the wedding of the happy lovers is described through her disdainful commentary: 'Very little white satin, very few lace veils; a most pitiful business! — Selina would stare when she heard of it.' Austen does not deny the fulfilment of the reader's fantasies, the desired end of all romances — 'the wishes, the hopes, the confidence, the predictions of the small band of true friends who witnessed the ceremony, were fully answered in the perfect happiness of the union'. The narrative suddenly changes perspective from the quite precise calendar of a year's events[1] to an indefinite present and future ('were fully answered' — when? at what point?). But the specific reality of Mrs Elton remains, popping up where she's least wanted, reminding us that 'perfection' does not come so soon — if at all — in the real world.

Conclusion

This study began with Mr Weston's crashingly inappropriate pun on 'Emma' as '*perfection*' and ended with the ironic qualifications with which Austen as narrator surrounds the image of the '*perfect happiness* of the union' of Emma and Mr Knightley. By concentrating on the novel's fascination with games and acting I have invited the reader to follow Jane Austen's own obsession with the moral complexities of her art. Throughout the fifty-five intricate chapters apparently describing the simple lives of '3 or 4 Families in a Country Village' Austen is also composing a *meta*-novel, a commentary on fiction itself. We have seen how in the Frank and Emma scenes, especially, the novel uses the conventions of theatre — acting out fictional stories for an adult audience — in order to criticise the notion that social game-playing is an appropriate way for adults to relate. We have seen how Austen deploys the conventions of romance in structuring her novel at the same time as she is critiquing the tendency of people to treat the phenomena of real life as though they were the elements of a romance. We have seen that she is happy to appropriate the anti-realistic tradition of allegory in order to give extra spiritual and political resonances to her story. And, perhaps above all, remembering that all readers of *Emma* were once 'first-time readers', we realise that Austen has written a novel which virtually demands to be read more than once, so that the 'second-time reader' may have the pleasure of watching the development of the secret plot, the romance between Frank and Jane, and its complex effect on the apparently simple goings-on of the people of Highbury. Yet this use of a secret plot (a precursor to the detective-story genre, not to be invented until some fifty years after Austen's death) is in order to demonstrate the moral truth stated with forthright simplicity by Mr Knightley:

> 'Mystery; Finesse — how they pervert the understanding! My Emma, does not every thing serve to prove more and more the beauty of truth and sincerity in all our dealings with each other?' (p. 404)

Mr Knightley is a character whose function in the novel is to represent the ideal, yet he is humanised by a certain emotional naiveté and by the unexpected storms of sexual jealousy that arise in him at the thought of Emma's interest in Frank Churchill. He also lacks the worldly irony of the narrator, who remarks on just this matter of the ideal of 'sincerity' in relationships,

> Seldom, very seldom, does complete truth belong to any human disclosure; seldom can it happen that something is not a little disguised, or a little mistaken; but where, as in this case, though the conduct is mistaken, the feelings are not, it may not be very material. (p. 391)

This perhaps could be read as Austen's final comment on the pleasures and perils of fiction: the novel, like all other 'human disclosures' — whether narratives or other utterances — cannot present the 'complete truth' about anything; but it can appeal to the right 'feelings' of its readers through the artful arrangement of its various disguises: characters, plot, verbal games, games with genre. *Emma* offers us complex pleasure, which *may* also — perhaps at first, perhaps on a third or fourth rereading — lead us to contemplate the great and eternal questions of good and evil in our doings with each other.

NOTES

Chapter 1

1 This is a family memory recorded in the *Memoir* by Jane Austen's nephew, J. E. Austen-Leigh, published in 1870 (reprinted in the Penguin edition of *Persuasion*, 1965, p. 376). The same page records the tradition that *pardon* was the 'collection of letters anxiously pushed towards' Jane by Frank, 'and resolutely swept away by her unexamined' after his insulting use of 'Dixon' in the alphabet game (p. 315).

2 John Wiltshire, *Jane Austen and the Body*, Cambridge University Press, 1992, p. 9. The Introduction and the chapter on *Emma* are well worth reading. On Mr Woodhouse and the Westons' wedding cake he comments, 'because it is to be eaten, and eaten with relish, it symbolises, in a more amplified fashion, the bodily enjoyments that Mr Woodhouse's mode of life is devoted to reducing. He resists all walks, outings, late nights, dances, trips, expeditions, excursions, engagements, marriages on the pretext that these activities endanger health. His programme is the denial of almost all bodily activity and almost all bodily enjoyment. ... He does not like to be reminded of the body's demands and appetites' (p. 126).

3 'Turnip Townshend', Charles, Second Viscount Townshend, retired from politics in 1730 in order to devote himself to improving agricultural methods.

Chapter 3

1 William Blake wrote his poem 'And did those feet', about building 'Jerusalem' in 'England's green and pleasant land' (though he wrote to counter the 'dark Satanic mills' of burgeoning industrialism) in the early 1800s. Jane Austen is unlikely to have read it, but the coincidence of the two writers' deeply felt vision of the English landscape is an interesting sign of the times. One of Jane Austen's brothers noticed her blossom in midsummer and teased her about it on publication of the novel, 'Jane, I wish you would tell me where you get those apple-trees of yours that come into bloom in July'.

Chapter 4

1 'Emma's interest in Harriet is not merely mistress-and-pupil, but quite emotional and particular: for a time at least. ... Emma is in love with her: a love unphysical and inadmissible, even perhaps undefinable in such a society; and therefore safe.' Mudrick in Lodge, p. 126. A real-life example of an Emma-and-Harriet relationship in the period is to be found in the diary of Anne Lister, *I Know My Own Heart*, ed. Helena Whitbread, Virago, 1988: Lister's affairs *were* physical, not at all 'undefinable', though the language in which she records them has its own euphemisms.

2 Readers interested in pursuing this matter of Jane Austen's use of the unconscious language of the body might like to consult my article 'The Romanticism of *Persuasion*', Sydney Studies in English, 5 (1979–80), pp. 15–30.

Chapter 5

1 Chapman offers a chronology of the events in *Emma* at the back of the Collected Edition, which demonstrates how carefully Austen worked to create a simulacrum of the 'real' world.

FURTHER READING

R. W. Chapman's authoritative Collected Edition of the Novels of Jane Austen (vol. IV, *Emma* with corrections by Mary Lascelles, OUP, 1966) is always worth consulting for its well-informed historical notes, its contemporary pictures, and its essays on such things as 'The Manners of the Age'. Volume VI, *Minor Works* (1954), offers many delights in Jane Austen's juvenilia, which are largely parodies of popular contemporary literature.

Jane Austen's Letters to her Sister Cassandra and Others were edited by Chapman in two volumes, OUP, 1932, with several subsequent revisions.

A good recent biography is Park Honan, *Jane Austen: Her Life*, Weidenfeld and Nicholson,1987; Deirdre Le Faye's revision of *Jane Austen: A Family Record* by W. and R. A. Austen-Leigh (The British Library,1989) is densely detailed and very authoritative.

Two books which supply answers to most factual queries about Jane Austen's life and times are *The Jane Austen Handbook* ed. J. D. Grey, Athlone Press, 1986; and *Jane Austen's Town and Country Style*, by Susan Watkins, Thames and Hudson, 1990 — this has many superb colour pictures.

Criticism

The following is a selection of books and articles published in recent years which offer a more exploratory and challenging reading of Jane Austen's novels than the standard appreciations of her art. A representative selection of the latter can be found in the Casebook edited by David Lodge, *Jane Austen: Emma* (Macmillan, 1968); this includes the chapter on *Emma* from Marvin Mudrick's *Irony as Defense and Discovery*. J. F. Burrows, *Jane Austen's Emma*, although published as long ago as 1968 (Sydney University Press), is an exemplary 'close reading' of the text, though it perhaps over-stresses Mr Knightley's jealousy.

Roger Gard, *Jane Austen's Novels: The Art of Clarity*, Yale University Press, 1992. The chapter on 'Emma's Choices' is a lively, witty, and thought-provoking reading of Austen's literary techniques.

Claudia L. Johnson, *Jane Austen: Women, Politics, and the Novel* , University of Chicago Press, 1988. A subtle and historically well-informed feminist reading.

David Monaghan (ed.) *New Casebooks: Emma*, Macmillan, 1992. Contains modern essays of great critical sophistication, and a useful 'Further Reading' section with commentary.

Leroy W. Smith, *Jane Austen and the Drama of Woman*, Macmillan, 1983.

Janet Todd (ed.), *Jane Austen: New Perspectives* (Women and Literature, New Series, vol.3), Holmes and Meier, 1983. Joel Weinsheimer's essay '*Emma* and its Critics' is a challenging consideration of critical attitudes to the novel.

John Wiltshire, *Jane Austen and the Body*, Cambridge University Press, 1992.